REDDENED WATER FLO‍

JEAN ARASANAYAGAM, born Jean Solomons into a comfortable Dutch Burgher family in what was then colonial Ceylon, is a Sri Lankan poet who describes herself as a writer 'suckled on a breast shaped by the genetics of history'. She attended a private Methodist Missionary school and obtained her B.A. degree English, Latin and History and her Diploma in Education from the University of Ceylon, Peradeniya. She earned an M.Litt in Literary Linguistics from the University of Strathclyde, Glasgow. Her experience in England and Scotland resulted in a collection of poems *Out of our Prisons we Emerge*. It was, as she comments, a e-exploration and re-discovery of a personal identity that had been buried beneath the overwhelming crisis of a country at war'. Yet she could never forget the life she would return to: 'Echoes of voices reach us even at this distance from the country of your birth and lie close within the ear even with those new ‍ces.'

Jean Arasanayagam has been seen as a poet of the bi-cultural experience and one who possesses a prophetic voice in viewing the tragic events of her country. Her themes also deal with her ancestral racial consciousneses and with her own personal and individual experience. 'I write poems which emerge out of my ‍ams, out of the subconscious or unconscious part of me. The ‍ate of my emotions has always provided subjects for my ‍iting. The subject of my identity in relation to colonialism and parallels in history . . . however my major pre-occupation has be‍ with the vast, the immeasurable tragedy of a country at war.'

Jean Arasanayagam is one of the leading all-English poets in Sri Lanka, having won the Sri Lankan Arts Council Prize for non-‍n (1984) with 'Bhairava: A Childhood in Navaly', the Sri an Arts Council Prize for Poetry with 'Apocalypse '83' ‍ly, 1985), and the Triton College International Poetry ‍d (1990). She is currently lecturing in English Literature at ‍nglish Teachers' College, Peradeniya.

‍ poetry has apperared in magazines in Sri Lanka, England, ‍ica, New Zealand, Sweden, Denmark, Japan, Australia and Among her books of verse are *Kindura* (1973), *Poems of a Beginning and a Season Over* (1977), *Apocalypse '83* (1984), ‍y Terror (1987), *Out of our Prisons we Emerge* (1987). She has ‍ published a collection of short stories *The Cry of the Kite* and ‍ novel *The Outsider*.

She is married to Thiagarajah Arasanayagam, writer, painter and playwright, and has two daughters who are themselves writers. She lives, works and writes in Kandy, and from her travels abroad she brings back her poems and stories.

Jean Arasanayagam

*R*eddened *W*ater *F*lows *C*lear

POEMS FROM SRI LANKA

by Jean Arasanayagam

FOREST
BOOKS
London & Boston

Introduced by
Norman Simms

PUBLISHED BY
FOREST BOOKS

20 Forest View, Chingford, London E4 7AY, UK
61 Lincoln Road, Wayland, MA 01778, USA

FIRST PUBLISHED 1991

Typeset in Great Britain by Cover to Cover, Cambridge
Printed in Great Britain by BPCC Wheatons Ltd, Exeter

ISBN 0 948259 96 5 ✓

British Library Cataloguing in Publication Data:
Arasanayagam, Jean
Reddened water flows clear: poems from Sri Lanka.
I. Title
821

Library of Congress Catalog Card No.:
90–82383

The publisher acknowledges the financial assistance of:
The Carnegie Trust for the Universities of Scotland
and the University of Strathclyde

Contents

Introduction

For Jean Arasanayagam language is a sensuous tool, a stylus that cuts deep into the wax of experience and leaves a trail of clear marks into which, all too often, runs the blood of the endless civil strife of her native Sri Lanka. Poetry of this sort cannot be measured simply on a scale of aesthetic values, as though the poet — or the reader — could choose to sit dispassionately in a gazebo, while the birds and insects sing in the lazy tropical afternoon. Yet a poetry that is merely sententious, engaged, and heavy with the odours of rotting corpses and burned out villages, will pale before the awesome and awful realities it refers to. Arasanayagam's strengths, rather, lie in her capacity to transmute the base metals of raw death and corroded culture into the pure gold of poetry: a poetry that neither cringes before politics and its extension into (civil) war nor deprives the victims of national catastrophe of their genuine groans and the silence of death; a poetry, in other words, which uses the tropes and figures of art to make into the illusion of sensuous words the things that otherwise belie the capacities of journalism, government reports, and fanatical propaganda to articulate.

Even when she does not write directly of the carnage that splatters its presence onto the landscape and consciousness of the teardrop-jewel island of Sri Lanka, Arasanayagam creates a language extending from poem to poem in order to enfold within the poems of history and the topographical, almost-pastoral verses the permeating and defining essence of the national emergency. Most of her poems are long, their structures loose in terms of any formal metres, stanzaic patterns, even verse-paragraphing. Yet the language is sensuous, sinuous, weaving images and themes into a tight fabric, a carpet of precisely spun threads closely bound, each strand immaculate with colour and tone, the whole fabrication emerging into pictures that hold the horrors of modern Sri Lanka and the exotic luxuries and homely details of Ceylonese history in a precarious and dynamic balance.

Aware of her mixed European heritage, Arasanayagam

deals with the Dutch colonial experience, the legacy of their paintings and architecture, in such a way that the reality of Burgher life forms one of the major strands in the cloth she is weaving. Colonialism is not dismissed into the facile rhetoric of ideologies, but scrutinized and transmogrified in the passions of poetic statement. The Dutch settlers came as individuals, engaged with other individuals, and both sets of persons recreated one another. Yet even that image is too simplistic for the complex web of finely-wrought silken threads in her poetry, as in the history of the island nation. For as the Sri Lankans are not one people, but now Tamils, Sinhalese and Burghers, with many subtle gradations between of regional groupings, so too the Dutch were not one homogeneous mass of oppressors and settlers. And after the Dutch came the British, who also interacted and interanimated, brought their culture, recreated their dreams and themselves, and departed other than what they were when they came and left part of their new and old selves.

That Arasanayagam is an artist as well as a poet may help to explain her interest in paintings and her painterly eye for detail in the poems. She writes about paintings by entering into them, touching them with the tongue and fingers as well as the eyes of her pen, so that the world and the canvas are reversed, we finding ourselves inside the painting peering out, if at all, at the cold fixed world of our normal perceptions. Even more, when the poet enters the canvas of the painting, she begins to rearrange, reanimate and re-define the experiences brushed on to the flat surface by the artist. Meanwhile, in most of the poems of description, the reader finds the words of poetry generating a tactile and tonal world of details, as though the world the poet desc-ribes were become a painting itself, and the very form of the exercise simultaneously recorded as in a documentary photograph the gruesome and harsh reality of massacre and disease and also instilled those images and sensuous phrases with what they lack in time's flux and the grief of the moment, namely, a sense of dignity in the victims and the culture to which they belong. Not a banal pseudo-tragic aura on the political issues or in the sewage of romantic and nationalistic slogans: but a dignity that inheres in the struggle of ordinary people to survive, to make sense of their lives, to keep hold of the memories they inherited of a more peaceful and purposeful way of living.

There is no glossing over of what is distasteful and no adolescent glorying in the agonies of a humiliated people. By such understated means as alliteration, assonance and rhythmic patterning the terms of unspeakable and unimaginable suffering become part of the fabric of poetry. How is this done without lapsing into banality? How is it that the poet's illusion does not collapse into forgeries? In a sense, as I have said, it is done by the dialectic of painting, the insides and outsides losing their strong difference, and the painterly details being applied not to mirrors — cold, hard, unyielding – but to strands of cotton or silk, woven into a tight-mesh of cloth, a carpet created in the very process of the poem. In another sense, it is done by the special presence of the poet's speaking voice, the controlling 'I' that moves from line to line, caressing the luxurious landscape, comforting the suffering victims, despising the acts of violence, neglect and despair. Still further, that 'I' acts as a needle pulling the thread of dignity-endowing sympathy through the harshness of the imaginary landscapes and paintings; and an 'I' which is also the needle on a gramophone, offering amplification to the muted sounds of the disenfranchised and the murdered, so that they speak through her articulated descriptions, her voice their persona, their mouthpiece. Here a short poem like 'The Stubborn Image' almost explicitly reveals the process:

> *Looking into mirrors we choose the image*
> *That stays with the dream, virginal, pure*
> *Uncorrupt, illusion's naive bride as if*
> *No contagion has ever touched the screen*
> *Of silver flesh, no pustulent sore that bursts*
> *Oozes and spreads a plague of lust*
> *That speaks of ravished death.*

But this is only a single, limited view, and the process revealed is only partly apt for all Arasanayagam's poetry. In many instances, her voice is more rhetorical, more strident, deliberately engaging reader or some external institution in debate, in a poetry whose tendency to harangue and satire, however, is checked by the unusual density of her poetic line, its sensuous images, its verbal complexity as it weaves together the insides and outsides of art and experience.

This scene of the poet's vision is crowded, thickly over-layed by images drawn not only from the landscapes of rural Sri Lanka and teeming cities (Glasgow, Delhi, Kandy) and the painting of the Dutch Masters and Renaissance portraitists, but also with the imagery of Hindu festivals, Latin epic poetry, modern political discourse, and the poet's own existential awareness of the female body as the site of sexual passion and the trauma of birth. Indeed, in many ways, like prisoners in Kafka's penal colony who have their crimes inscribed on them with a grotesque needle-machine, so the very body of Sri Lanka seems often to be a female torso tattooed by the pen of politics and warfare:

> *Coughs gulf through in spasms of thick phlegm*
> *Women hunch over creep back foetal into wombs*
> *Of pain gestate themselves pushing tears and gasping*
> *Breath into their unclenching palms*
>
> (Ward 31)

It is this identification of the flesh-and-blood image of the land as the body of a woman that seems to allow Arasan-ayagam to speak the experience of current events in the language of the intricacies of jungle plants, animals, villages:

> *We are all travelling through endless forests*
> *Of pain, routeless paths and the darkness of leaves*
> *And trees lurch into your body, football*
> *Knocking against stone hearing the rustle of*
> *The death serpents under the scroll of ferns*

The jungle ticks fastening into your flesh
Hopping off the wounded beasts
As they follow the bloodied spoor.

(Ward 31)

It is through this intrusive, invasive presence of the outside world of pain and suffering, sometimes explictly and sometimes implicitly caused by the madness of human agency, that the pen cuts into the flesh of the woman's body, penetrates the places of pleasure and generation, and leaves on the surface of the skin, the text of the poem, like the canvas of a painting or elaborate needlework, which as we have said earlier, is the zone of transmogrification, of interinanimation (to use John Donne's word), where art and experience recreate each other, where agony and dignity meet, meld, and generate the poems we here set before the reader. By this means, the surface ceases to be an exterior boundary between inside and outside. The text of the poem is at once the interface of art and experience, but only superficially so; for the text more so is content, substance, the created and creating experience of an artistic trans-formation of Sri Lanka's physical ordeal into a bold state-ment of its cultural dignity. The body of suffering is the body of the poet's writing. Even a poem without political points of reference, like 'Puberty rites', develops the larger image of the female body weaving in and out of the darker, more sobering visions of a nation destroying itself.

The portrait Arasanayagam paints is also a palimpsest in another sense, a chronological one. She views the events of the present emergency through a perspective glass that is not innocent of its own stains and carnage. While she and her fellows were being educated at home and in festivals and in the schools run by foreigners, Europeans, her island nation seemed pure, aloof from the horrors that run like a red thread through the history of European civilization. That seeming purity, however, disappeared as the horrors crystallized in her own day-to-day experience. Then the present crisscrossed with the counter-texts of ancient epic poetry with its glorification of war and its ritual celebrations of sacrifice, and even the apparently pastoral customs of the countrside were stained with the gore of the hunt and blood sports. Once the pretence to innocence is gone the whole of Sri Lankan history may be seen as already always a wide tangled skein of violence and violation. Hence she says, in one poem:

> *We share the same guilt*
> *We were once invaders*
> *Whether Commandant, predikanten*
> *Conquistador or Koopman*
> *On our brows eating into skull*
> *We bear branded the mark of Cain.*
> > (A Question of Identity)

Ironically, she does not explore the implications of that last allusion to the mark of Cain. She sees it as a brand placed on the body of the first murderer, fratricide. It is for her a mark which, since we are all at once our brothers' keepers and our brothers' killers, defines the human experience. Yet the God of Genesis placed it on Cain to separate him and protect him from human revenge, not to stigmatize him as a scapegoat for all the ills of our race. Arasanayagam's God seems little interested in such niceties, however. In one sense, this God is the mangled corpse of Christ forever suffering on the Cross, a microcosmic embodiment of the human condition, the focal point of all those cumulative little pains that add up to universal agony. In another sense, God is the Logos of Creation who 'turned the world into a charnel house', the power and authority of the State and all the state forces in the world trained on to the body of the universal victim; eternal artist who chisels bones into the corpse of this world.

> *Naked they bathe in the springs*
> *wipe the bone clean of blood*
> *let the sap seep slowly back within*

the marrow feel the water gush
through rock, cleanse the flesh
that has long been polluted by
the stench of death bare their
wounds to the sun, red flowers
that stunned the dark now fade with light,
blood leaps and dances,
the reddened water flows
clear, their folded shadows
unfurl themselves and lengthened
stretch upon the whole strand . . .

(Naked They Bathe)

If it does not happen that we can pursue the cultural contexts to Arasanayagam's biblical allusions, it is not because she is unread in Scriptures or European literature; no more so than she is ignorant of Hindu and Buddhist classics. The matrix of her poetry lies not in the embedded written texts, though she often will draw from them names, places, themes, concerns. The heart is in the vibrant, quivering flesh of the living body of Sri Lanka, an organic presence in her verse, and a parchment of flesh on which she inscribes her poetry.

In many ways, though, Arasanayagam's writing fits within the textures of European modernism, as her allusions to Baudelaire and the Surrealists makes evident. Her writing is saturated with the post-Romantic sensibilities of those poets who seek to devour the world of the senses in the seething web of their words, who weave a thick mat of language to encompass the unspeakable and unimaginable truths of private experience. Yet she does more than interweave that fabric with the textures (and alluded to texts of Sri Lankan poetry and ritual), though, of course, that happens as well. She also deconstructs those forms and modes of prior textuality, and using a poetic speech that washes profusely out of the wounds in the corpus of those foundational discourses, she flows beyond the limits of speech and imagination. Why? Because, as we indicated before, the trauma of the violence which now pervades and begins to define the life-experience of Sri Lanka silences all previous talk and occludes traditional means of seeing. Or if that trauma does not destroy fully, it destroys the validity, and enforces a condition where normal (normative) discourses must be held under erasure. Words must be spoken and scenes described but we can no longer trust our tongues or our eyes, and each word we speak or picture we imagine must be quickly replaced by another.

What is important then is not the precise poetic statement, the well-turned phrase or well-made metaphor. It is the flow of discourse, the new discourse of poetry traumatized by massacres, bombs, disruptions to normal life. Thus every thing that is spoken or seen seems at once familiar and revalorized, made strange by the urging of poetic energy, the desperate need to put into words an experience beyond the processes of conceptualization. From this process emerges the brilliance of Jean Arasanayagam's writings in lines as striking and soul-reorientating as these:

> *Biting into apples clenched with rounded colour*
> *I taste the ash of my body in flowering flesh*
> *That's soon ready, beneath the sun for spoiling*
> (The New Journey)

Anyone who can write like this deserves to be read, and the collection of verse which follows enfolds the reader in a brace of such lines to the extent that we know we are in the presence of a new and powerful, commanding voice of late twentieth century poetry.

Norman Simms
Hamilton
New Zealand

xiv

The Poems

This new journey *India 1986–7*

Coming back to rediscover familiarity
I find the flowers have not changed
Their colour nor their fruit but the taste
On my tongue is different an amalgam
Of acrid urine staling in the sun and newly
Opened jasmine buds soon festering flowers
That streak my hair and wound my neck
With garlands in celebration of either life or death

Biting into apples clenched with rounded colour
I taste the ash of my body in flowering flesh
That's soon ready, beneath the sun for spoiling

The familiarity of a landscape recurs
And roads run through the fields of my brain
That I know must lead somewhere, already
Mapped by other lives and others' histories
This time at least I know where I am going
If not what I am searching for
Temples where stones, silent as death
Spread arms lift feet in Siva's
Tandava dance, stir to life
The sleeping lids, ankles stamp
The puny earth with quakes that shiver
Into shattering the gungru bells
To crush underfoot the evil asuras

Bathed and chanted to with ghee
And sandlewood the stone takes on
The colour of the ritual flesh
Limbs swathed in silk and threads of gold
Become god to him who prays
For crooked limbs to straighten
Or for frenzies to grow calm as
Sedated rivers flowing through the
Vulture-hovering plains trickling
Like spittle from tongues of drought
Licking the salt of parching earth

3

On this journey the dark comes swiftly
The horns shoot into waking the wayside
Sleeping huddles, hands move curtains
Of dreams that split into pooja halves
Of coconuts, find no milk taste ash and juice
Upon the starving tongues that lap the
Drying rivers of their prayers

Bus-loads alight to urinate into the night
Seek shadows by a wall or growing tree
Figures from flat silhouettes of shadowed
Screens emerge and speak, 'Do not pollute
Our dreams, the wind blows the smell
Towards our doors, how can we sleep?
Go elsewhere do not come here
Let the dust settle, let us smell
The cooling earth.'

The hot sweat pours from new apertures
In my flesh to mingle with the dust
From unknown streets trellised with sun-
Baked shadows hollowed into long necked jars
Lead you into cool courtyards and rooms
Where sacked bodies store their lives like grain
Before crushed kernels in their mounds are
Measured and weighed in scales
To feed our beggared mouths
Outside the woven huts
Alponas press upon the earth
The twisting tongues that speak
An esoteric language to the gods
To call rain for the fields
Fruit for the branch

I stand and watch the flesh of Meenakshi
Growing fragrant with fruit and juice and
Sandlewood while human flesh

Opens with sores red as the roses from
Threaded garlands to beg the street
I leave them thronged praying at a tree
Which opens breasts with milk, then becomes
A deity swathed with a saffron cloth
Garlanded, bathed with sandlewood
Milk that comes from blood that soaks
Its roots and turns wood into flesh
And flesh again becomes the supernatural tree

I retch the sun from my guts and pour
Libations from the earthen water pots
Upon my parching tongue

A blind man playing ragas upon the flutes
Of night sings into my ear while rats
With bloodied mouths flung from their traps
Lie upon the pavements of my tread
The fires burn to roast and sizzle
Man's hunger in their pans and on their spits
The city fries and broils in spluttering
Oil that shapes of breast and phallus
As hunger roams upon the streets
To end up on a cart, piled fish
The piercing bone crisped with burning
Flesh lie flat or dangle,
Gulping and feeding, tongues, fingers,
Bellies grip and tear into the grain
And meat

We arrive. A sleeping guide unfolds
His shade withdraws his darkness
From steps of lodging house. We follow
'We want hotel,' we say. 'I know hotel.
I take you.' Saleem Travel Agency
Ablaze with light. Sleek with gold and jewelled
Rings teeth and smiles flash. We sit gazing
At fellow travellers each gazing into his
Own mirror of tiredness.

'Sister, sit down. Sister, first please sit.
You want room? We have family room
Double room. Extra bed. We charge sixty-five
Rupees.'
'We are tired. We want to rest
You will give us a room?'
'Sister, six o'clock we give you room.'
'Can we have some hot tea, please,
We are told that Bangalore tea is the best.'
'Acha, that is true.
In Tamilnadu Kafi is best
Here tea is very good.'
'Here, bring tea. Sister, never mind
You give money later.
You can have hotel room at six o'clock.
Till then, sister, sit down please. Take rest.
Now, sister, we have tours, Bangalore
Mysore, Ooti — You must see Nilgiries
Famous Brindavan Gardens with fountains
All lit up and buy Mysore silk, Sandlewood
Everything . . .'
Hundreds of rupees to be paid
To see what we would rather
Discover for ourselves, make our
Own explorations

'Sir, can I speak with you one minute
You are taking tour with us? Here is receipt.'

'No, all we want is a room
We prefer to make our own journeys.'
Faces fall. The rooms are full

'There are no rooms. You go to other hotel.'
We search again.
'Common bathroom. That hotel not good.
I take you to Voyshella. That good hotel.'
'No, take us to Hotel Tourist
We will try to find room there.'

6

'Then you pay me double fare.
Double fare because you hire at night.'
'But six o'clock is not night.'
We end . . . here.

We end up in Hotel Tourist
Pour brass chembus of water on our limbs
Unpack our dreams, unroll maps
From our minds, chart the route to palaces,
Temples of fables and myths, we become
Legends to ourselves and draw our lives
In frescoes on those walls already crowded
With gods and goddesses where briefly we lose
Our way, abandoning the tramping of those streets
As refugees from bombs and burning houses

Return.
Watching video in the bus
Am I expected to weep
At a heroine pricked and pierced
By crabs scuttling over her voluptuous body
Clap hands when the villain is shot
Through shutes into their crawling melées?

'We are now approaching place named Tipu Palace
You see gambaz of Tipu Sultan, Hyder Ali,
Fatima Begum
Here also place where Tipu Sultan body found
Killed by Captain Harry,' says the guide
On the bus to Mysore, ghosts we search for
An empty plot and ruins while tourists wonder
Over the smooth lawns
'We also see Brindavan Gardens in
Place named Mysore, now we approaching,
For my services you pay rupees two
See the Brindavan Gardens
Six-thirty bus sharp is leaving
We are not taking responsibility
If you not come in time

Not buses to Bangalore also that time.'

'We will not pay
He is useless guide
He could not speak English also
We are not understanding one word he said'

Pin drop silence.
'You are students only,' says the guide
'Put on the video. Put on the video.'
The blazered students with Public School
Crests settle back, notes put away
To watch unreal wars, titillating embrace.

What pilgrimage is this that takes me
Through this new journey to remake
Fresh acquaintance with the ancient gods
And ask for nothing? I make
No new vows nor do I ask for answer
To those prayers once clamoured for

Spices, essence of rose, the cloying flesh
Of sweet fragrances from flowers, odours
From sewers enter my nostrils my ears fill
With sacred songs and chants and prayers
As I wander in search from city
To city from street to street watching
My flesh change shape
My skin singe in scorching sun
My skin tattooed with memory
Leaves not one inch to be pricked
With fresh design and colour,
My feet covered with dust
Journeys where others have reincarnated
Their steps through endless roads
Of birth, rebirth through life to death
To pyres now lit not on the banks of
Sacred rivers but where the bodies
Burn in rites of war.

Departure from the village

I stand holding rice in my palm from the last
Paddy harvest, picking out the polished stones
Of hard edged memory that threaten to lodge
Between the teeth with each mouthful ladled off
The pot, taking the edge off appetite, yet
Making me remember that once the harvests were
Full and rich, milk rice laid out on plantain leaves
For the deities in propitiation

Now we must prepare to leave the fields fallow
For the new occupants to implant their seed
We have reaped our harvests appeased our hungers
No longer bow to any gods in supplication

Others too have known departures, others too have
Gone away, never to return, marched with the stars
Spun wildly with the brilliant constellations
Watched a waning or a waxing moon that made
The ocean waters restless with disquiet
Dwindling into a sickle scything the stars
Or growing rounded wide as open cave mouth
Flooded with light, yet when darkness came
Held torches blazing, of dried coconut fronds
So that we do not step on danger where the
Serpent coils.

It is nothing new to prepare here for parting
Or departure as gunshot once more sweeps over
The fields and with perhaps the last pluck
The coconuts fall hard, body blows thudding
On the bare earth as the man shins up the
Trunk, vertical, wall lizard climbing, his ankles
Rope noose strung, twisting the knotted stalk of
The green husked coconuts to fall tumbling
On the grass

9

We remember the falling bodies wrapped
In mat blood flung into the trenches among
The teak trees while the echo of gunshot
Struck hard against the rock fortress of Yapahuwa

The sky grows distant, out of reach as mountains
Fall, pile on fields that turn to ash filled graves
From the burnings of old and finished harvests

You pick up the coconuts, shake them closely
To the ear, feel thirst gurgling in the bellycave
Slash open the lid, placing your parched lips
To its mouth drinking like desert traveller in
Mirages of unquenched thirst

The pyramids of green nuts grow tall, left
In the sun until the carts come to take them
Away,

Sometimes the split husks lie strewn
The still damp fibres buzzing with mosquitoes
The silk white londa scooped out of the nut
And flung among the folded shafts of sleeping
Nidikumba.

CANTO II

We remember that yesterday has a flavour still
Unwrapping memory like roasted batagoyas
From sheathes of green habarala leaf, the flesh
Tasting high from their gunshot wounds
The slight taste of putrefaction and decay
Makes us gourmets of death, offers titillation
To our jaded tongues that had lost their salt

10

We break off piece after piece of kurakkan
Cakes baked stone hard on the kabala
Feeling hunger inside the belly groan like
A starving hyena that smelt flesh and licks
The dry rock where the deer has slept,
Set those rounded cakes, palm flat raban spinning
As they twirl in the dark skullminds
Lifting them on the thin whirling canes
Balanced on forehead or fingertip
Dizzying the air with our skill;
Now we lack agility, let the raban slip
Off, fall in a drunken faltering on the ground
Before it rests, place a slow hand to the bent
Spine, pick them up with trembling hand

CANTO III

Now we are parched with drought
The dogs loll about in the ash heaps singeing
Their fur, the flies settle on their flicking ears
And the fleas nip their thin flesh
Lean as strips of sundried venison

'On the other side', Mohotha says, 'the wild
Elephants, the deer and the wild boar are there still.'
But faraway as if the forest has moved with them.
'The jungles are all cut down
We have not had rain for two years
Our bodies are dried husks,
Hollow nuts without water,
Our trees have not borne coconuts
For the drought, it was a long time
Since I took a gun and walked
Into the forest.'

CANTO IV

Gillan squatting on his haunches on the earthfloor
Of the kitchen scoops out the slime of olu mud
From the guts of the loola fish with woodash
And the baskets of olu tubers in their tight
Black hairy sheaths from the wewa are brought
In for us to boil and peel
It is here that the womenfolk bathe in the evening
The kalagedis bobbing on the surface among olu and nelun
With a hand that sweeps the water drops off their faces
Their hair streaming behind them.

We cracked wood-apples on the sharp stones
And sucked out mangoes, the juices streaming down
Thickly golden, a lava of nectar on the craving hills
Of our flesh; the thick white milk boiled and frothed over
In the soot blackened udders of the full pots
Spilling over the hearthstones at the auspicious hour;
The thalagoyas crept into the garden and the hyena packs
Searched out the plumed jungle cocks

Dreams were a wandering through mazes
Of beak stitched weaver bird nests, feeling
The soft cobwebby fleece against the sleeping cheek
And the grain woven mats with their thick packed
Strands were pecked by the sparrows as they flew in
Streaming with golden kernels, Diwale offerings to the gods

We were all marauders, fed and thirsted
Satiate with the land its plenty, grew fat
As leeches in the rain-soaked grasses, grew
Glistening new reptilean skins, lifting jewelled
Hoods over the sprouting new paddy on the kamatha
Rifled the grain in the bissas, slept in rooms
Stacked with gunny bags of paddy from the harvests

12

CANTO V

Semasinghe is dead and his wife
Both are dead, their hut has caved in
The ribs shake hollow, the mud walls
Have shed their flesh sliding off into
The graves, crumbling into a handful or two
Of chena ash, now where they lie buried
The pumpkin vine will grow fat and the dried
Chillies lifted off the mat crackle under the
Grinding stone, smarting the tongue and making
The eyes bulge out,

The ebony koora that bound Semasinghe's
Long black hair, its roots nourished by oil
Simmering with herbs, slips off in thin white
Strands from the unravelling knot of his kondè;

Gillan is dead, his tomb in the next field to ours
And his wife no longer comes walking swiftly over
The nyere bearing the covered plates of honey-rich
Vali-thalapè,

My father's flute is silent, the antlers and snake-
Skins stripped off the walls, the guns put away
The new hunters do not need the cover of dark
The cover of the forest, as they walk openly with
Their guns cocked, they do not set snares but
Point their guns, take aim, without fear
At their prey as they pause
In their tracks

CANTO VI

We are now ready to relinquish her,
Our mother earth, walk off bereaved
Having fed from her, used her, sucked until

13

The nipples clenched themselves against tongue
And teeth, now with dessicating flesh we carry
The depleted kuruni baskets of our lives
With the remnants of the last repast
Packed in for the final journey

We fling the empty leaf aside
The residue of bones scatter and feel the old
Hunger return, the craving, the thirst for the kiul
Water sweetened with root of eramusu

As we walk away leaving the field unploughed
Already the new occupants take over, holding
Their guns unmuzzled towards us

We watch our lives shrivelling up, dying
Grasshoppers in drought, rustling in the dry grass
And remember the fat loolas floating under
The nelun flowers before the water reddens
Again, with blood.

Destroying an enemy

Semasinghe Mudiyanse of Mahawa speaks . . .

At dawn I arose
The sky the colour of the streaked
Underwing feathers of the batagoya
Flying over the still pale waters of the Mahawewa
Mist trickling over the coconut fronds
The grass wet heavy and white
With feverish dews

I recited the mantras learned
From my gurunanse
Prepared the gotuwa with cooked food
Goda mas, diya mas and five kinds
Of puluthu, mung and thala from the chena
Paddy from the field by the tamarind tree
Where nightly the nariyas' cries hang
Shivering like dangling knife blades
Scraping against the dark,
From the other side of the Mahawewa
The hunters brought wild boar and venison,
Loola fish from the olu filled waters,
My woman gutted and cleaned
With ash, no taste of mud remained
In the flesh threaded by fine
Silver bones, cooked and wrapped
In fresh leaves

We journey in the railway
A long journey to the South
I smelt the sea on my palms
My skin itched with salt
My eyes crawled dazzled with fish
A silver net dangling before my eyes

15

We arrived there
The woman read the anjanan eliya
She told us who the enemy was.
I prepared the dehi tinduwa
Arranged the twenty four betal leaves
Like flower petals, sliced the arecanut
Finely with the giraya

The red necklace of blood
Peered out of the feathers
Of the black sacrificial cockbird
I shook the driplets off the screeching
Knife blade, swallowed fire
Spewed out sparking gushes of flames
As I danced

We threw the gotta on the other side
Of the fence, on this side the Veda's fence
On the other, his enemy's
We returned after three days

Meanwhile that house caught fire
The thatch burnt quickly, being very dry
Like unoiled hair, combed by flames
I did not see the face of the enemy

I came back to the house
On the banks of the Mahawewa
The jungle was then full of wild boar
Deer, bear and leopard, the woodapples
Ripening inside their shells, slowly,
The thalagoya crawling in the garden
And the nidhanaya guarded
By the great naga that lives by the kamatha,
The bissa was full

We have fed the gods with milk rice
Renewed the thatch of our roof

The great drought will soon come
And the coconuts grow small
Their water meagre on the stunted trees
The loola fish burrow deeper into the moist
Mud and the time of sickness comes

The paddyfields burn in the heat
The animals have retreated further
Into the vestigious forest
When I was young my hair was heavy
Black and long, it was tied in a knot
Skewered with an ebony koora
My father simmered pots of oil
With herbs and seeds to nourish its roots

My hair is now white
Strand by strand I comb and coil
It round my palm
I lose count of the days
The ribs of my mud hut show
Its starveling age and the mati walls
Are slowly crumbling like the betel nut
That I pound in the mortar
But the thumbases are still strong

It was there in the teak forests
We heard the sound of gunshot
They dug their own graves
Fell into them, the young teak trees
Are growing there again, the saplings
Whose roots drank blood

My sons now sow the fields
My brother Gilan's tomb lies
Where the harvests spring up
The waulas drop the small mee-amba
Among the piled coconuts after the picking
Ravaging the trees at night

The mongoose and the serpent
Confront each other, locked in battle
Scorpions and centipedes creep
Rustling into the husks

It grows dark early
There is no water left
To catch the light that falls
From the sky canopy
The eyes of the blind olu
Are buried in slime

The death bird flies
Over the fields
Gunshot sounds again
But the hunters are now grown old
Their flintlocks rusty, asleep in their huts

My wife's fingers that once wove small mats
For the Diwale offerings are now stiff
The golden straw was then the colour
Of her skin

Death is the great black mapila
That rustles under the folded mat.

Primeval Forests

Ohiya 1982

Great trees' bark thick like singed flesh
Perfectly scarred to beauty circled with
Deep ringed gaping ridges
Brimming with resin blood,
Eucalyptus, spruce, conifers black-green
Branching out like out-thrust tusks,
Through thunder-dark cages and caverns
We travel in our panic passage,
So small we are, so human,
Clamouring to reach, with throbbing nerves and pulse,
Wide plains that stretch to white horizons,
Windswept heaths soft-brushed and bleached
With light that spills from cloudless skies,
Thread through the grass a curving finger
Of water tracing its passage through the
Downs and so we come to forests of ferns
And flowers, wind chill at the lips we drink
Pure from the air, its moisture . . .
    Water in silence water among leaves,
    Grasses that grow and die and shed their seed
    And grow and perish into loam, black
    Dense crumbling pitted with white moss-like spores,
    Water in silence flowing in streams in deep
    Down gullies cutting a route through earth
    Piled rich with plants, trees, vines thick
    And twining rising from hidden source
    And bubbling springs,
Dark water sounds, voices that touch the rock
To speak down buried deep travelling through
Ancient bedrock where from germinal seed
Spring natural forests, arching branch and flower,
Where tree becomes stone and fish
Change fins in this miraculous age,
Calling from ferns, the mating cries of birds that
Sound from thick seas of grass and twisted

Rhododendron hung with spagnum moss,
Secret water flows beneath the web of vines
And creepers, prinnias whirr, flute whistle of
Arrenga pierces the gelid air. Water gurgling
Spilt from goblets of the earth to fall from
Boulders in froth filled streams, no image
Of the sky; no human eye can see what
Lies beneath this ancient bed teeming with
Mythic plant, bossed leaves clenched fists
Unfurled and tawny furred spider stems of fern,
Ancient, ancient the speech of nature,
Only the calling bird, the sound of water
And mists blowing down from clouds
Obscuring footpaths to the elk-filled
Wilderness — open this slight aperture
Into time . . .

God puts alms into the hands of beggars

God puts alms into the hands of the beggar
Into their emptiness the rich grain pours
His share of the apportioned harvests, his
Hands pluck the grape, spill the plenitude
As he measures out bushel after bushel
So that where it falls, the seed takes root again

He who receives now his beneficence, fields
That the thieves had ploughed, harvests they had
Garnered, now bestowed once more upon the heirs
God thinks rightful so that he will never know
Hunger again where the belly knocked hollow
As the finger tapped against its slack drum
The guts limp lampwick crying for oil
To feed its flame,

The beggar whose racked bones
Put forth petals of plush flesh all rosy
With blood warmth and fulness while the
Ambrosial nectar gilds the mouth and fills
The fissured tongue cracks with the juices of
Seasonal fruit, the teeth ripping off the skin
To suck dry to the stone all the honey that brims,
Feed flesh, quench thirst and the fish
Silver with oil lie on heaped platters bellies
Packed with seed pearls of white roe
Where you had slunk off cringing from the
Cleared bones thrown from the feasts,

Now you return to the banquet and sit
At the head of the laden table
Passing round the wine chalice to your neighbour
Replenished over and over again
You leave finally, the ambalama of your life
Where you rested from your wanderings
The rain beating in to shred your mat
The fires grown cold as you prepare to leave

And the three stones on which you set your pot
With plucked herbs and cold water, covered with grey
Crumbling death ash and a few pulled out
Half charred fire sticks left behind to be re-kindled
By the next wayfarer, no longer at night
Your crouching shadows livid scar
Grows like a crack in the wall through which the gecko
Creeps in pursuit of mate and food
Your dreams fold their thin shapes into nut slivers
Within the betel leaf tucked into
The meagre waist band of your hope

No longer the scarecrow frightens away
The birds while the sun dried roughened straw tickles
And grates against those outspread weatherbeaten
Hands with twisted knuckles that knock against
The heavy stalk and the stream now runs clear
Where you washed your muddied feet and lifted
In your cupped palm water to quench your thirst

Your arms grow heavy as branches bearing
Ripe fruit your life the harvest field swelling
And rustling with golden serpent coils of grain
The heavy sieves on the threshing floor lifted now
By willing hands winnows the chaff and the kindling
Gathered to nourish the simmering pot
With roaring flames

You take your ease on the new spread mat
Feel the shape of fingers unweave their braids
The straw smooth as oil rippling under your body
The roughness flaked away
Already the sparrows fill the pot with wisps
Of straw and the old serpent sheds its shard
As it creeps away from the mouldering thatch
That waits to be renewed.

Ancestors

It is so easy to say that one's ancestors
Were degenerate or exploiters or that they were
The lazy hoboes of the seaboard smoking their
Long pipes from morning to night their vision swathed
In a haze of tobacco, reeked of gin sipping it
Like mother's milk, their tables laden with dish
After dish of hot spiced Rijstafel and slaves
Supplying the status quo of their household,
Their rubicund wives sallying forth in satin
And velvet to listen to the sermons of the predikanten,
Cooling their foreheads beaded in sweat with palm
Fans and seeing God in his Calvinistic heaven
Dressed in the velvet cloak of the Elders
With a froth of ruffles at his throat and cherubim
Hovering among sober grey clouds with pearls in their
Earlobes while Satan sweated in the underworld
Barebodied like a pagan stoking his roasting fires
Waiting to go back home and dip their fingers
Into the fruitbowls while the mestizo slaves
Tickled their frizzed fringes and eased into
Slippers their kneaded feet sleeping away history
In long trellised dreams of hot afternoons

Yet it is with a kind of wonder
That I gaze at pictures of their flagships
And gallant Indiamen sail billowing
Find that they did not lack courage
Dared venture out on swelling oceans
Setting out from some European port
In kermis season when the canals
Slid along with skaters on iced marble
As the sea heaved unrolling the heavy parchment
Maps measuring the constellations with their
Astrolabes expecting sea monsters and mermaids
To jettison out of spouting fountains of green brine
— Find that although the seafarers rotted with scurvy
And perished of their bloody fluxes, ate beef
Nibbled already by salty maggots, survived;

— Aboard, a motley of wenches trying their luck
In the new lands, maidens from orphanages
To colonize the new territories with their blood,
   Their motives were trade and commerce,
      While they watched the stars reeling
      And dolphins disport themselves

Spent their guilders in the sixteenth-century bordels
And stripteases freed from the continence of long
Voyages, they dared as I have not, to risk all,
Unsure even of return to any earthly harbour
Slung their bones on any soil building with fleshly
Bricks their forts and factories, schools and kirks
And cemeteries

Soaked in sea brine bone weary slept in their
Hammocks while the huge obscene shapes of cargo
Rats scuttled in the dark hole with their stench
Of urine and faecal matter —

Had guts, saw land even in mirages and islands
Where spring water gushed through rock and scrawny
Chickens roasted on spits while fruits strange to
Their taste laved the mouth and tongue

Perhaps found strange men with eyes growing
Out of their sides and heads quivering with spiky
Green snakes

Most of this is true, I peer into their households
Their journeys through the voyeurism of history
Find that my eyes look out of those portraits
Of their genealogies

My ancestor was perhaps one of them
Staggering on a heaving deck looking
Forward to the fresh fruitpluck on the island

The hot sweat turning chill in his cloak
Of stained wool, sea chest bouncing on a heave
Of waves looking forward to a rich ring
With gems bright as winking yellow cockerel eyes
Waiting to dip his quill pen into new ink basins
Write the names of his progeny for history

That man, somewhere my ancestor whose name
Intrigues me slumbers in immortality
Since I will not let him die completely
He leaves some record flowing from his Calvinistic
Loins, a whole terrain copulate with what tenacity
The hybrid growth of his seed flowering
Into this strange foliage, nourished by this soil

If I am persistent enough I'll find new facts
To collaborate the evidence of his tenantship
And new roots for his vineyard, cull the harvest
Of his grape black with richness in wineskins of
Plenty, yet I have my times of drouth and then
Famished grasp the clustering fruit that burst
From udders of juice, find the wine sour.

Who was he? Living in some southern maritime
Port, never to go back with the spice cargoes
Or ivory, chank, gems and dyeroot
Engaged perhaps in private trade, found
Somewhere a woman whom he wived, begot
His offspring, named them with the good Dutch
Names which mixed with different bloods
Lost with time their flavour, yet took on
New colour

How many changes of clothes did he have
For that long sea voyage and how many guilders
Clinked in his pouch? Did his wife learn how
To make suikebrod and poffertjes and wafel
The doughcakes rising in the breudher pans

25

Or did they make do with salt fish and country
Rice washed down with the local brews,
Did she weave lace or coil her hair in braids
Sleeked with coconut oil,
She was a Dutch mevrouw — her name was
Elizabeth de Zeilve, had her own stamboek
Pure Dutch, came from Punta de Galle . . .

South

On the shore the fishermen empty their nets
It's a catch of small fish, in size about a finger's
Length. From among them a large fish slithers out
Silver as light caught and lifted as the sun
A wave of shimmering into air, black pointillist
Dots brushed on, on sharply sabre scales

Flung out on the sand it struggles
Blood and salt brine mixing in its guts

The fisherman who travels with the moon
Whose boat is drawn by twisting ropes
Of currents, he who knows shipwreck as the sky
Piles high with thunderous mountain clouds
Rifted by slashing blades of gutting knives
Of lightning, knows too compassion, takes the black
Silver fish by deathconch pointed eyes swirling
In dazzling cones of white sheened shell,
Lifts it, throws it back into the sea

The waves are not deep enough here, where his
Feet touch the undulant frills of white froth
So he wades out beyond the shallows and flings it
Into deeper waters

Weakly it begins to swim out further
Into the unnetted ocean

'It is poisonous for people to eat
Its belly gets distended
And turns blue.'

Yes, the fisherman too knows compassion;
He prays four times with folded hands pointing prayers
Like his own frail craft towards the waves
Pushing his body's vessel out upon the ocean
Prays to bring home a day's good catch,
Also for protection

Seeks in the deepening dusk, Christ
Walking in a glimmer on the waves and from

His hunger and his thirst is saved
By the giant turtle that appears out of the deep
Seabelly to feed him and his friends
With the miraculous manna, bread and wine
As he drifts out lost upon the ocean,
By night wrapped in sea vapour's dewy sail,
By day sucked dry as sea washed shell
Until he reaches rescue on those shores
So far away . . .

Women, goddesses and their mythologies

And how does she see me now, her throat
Empty of gold, like mine, yet her earlobes studded
Still with blood drop rubies brilliants — teardrop gems unshed
Her white and widowed hair, its parting once streaked
Thick with bright vermilion, now bereft of marriage symbol
Tracing through their sparse strands, a bare and lonely path,

How does she see me now, the one whose breath
Made the flames flicker, dwindle, almost die
On the altar of her gods, darkening with shadow
Their flawless skins oiled and bathed in milk and sandalwood
Their chiselled lips that smiled benignly, on her fortunes
And their waywardness, capricious gods that see the flesh
Slide off like shadow from a skeletal frame; kneeling
Before them, she turns on me a countenance of silence,
An apparition wreathed in incense that spins and spirals
In the air in swathes of fragrant smoke, veils that no one
Reft for fear of revelation, drifting miasmic from the
Burning pyres of dreams towards Kailasa, as if my prayers
And pleadings never should reach, even in whisper, to the
Ears of unknown deities that heard insistent the chantings
Of her interminable thevarams and mantras, her carnal loves
Through age, displaced by bakthi as she fasted — left her
Lord's bed empty, prayed and fed the hungry crows,

Allowed me once, but barely once to enter the sacred
Room, gaze upon her shrine with saints and gurus
And fold my hands in worship to those unknown gods
On whom she showered love, those goddesses of wealth
And learning, those powerful deities whose towering lingams,
Curling trunks, lotus and veenas inhabited the world
Of her sacred legends and mythologies, where I, with
Human limbs and eyes, whose sacrifice of blood fell
On those empty stone altars where not one single god
Would turn its eyes, belonged not to a single of her rituals,
Yet I entered, treading uncertain and wavering with
Naked sole, my feet, now unpolluted, washed and bathed
In turmeric, first having shaken off the dust of many

Journeys on roads and streets I trod, before this
Respite beckoned me, to halt, groping through darkness
For hands of fire to lead me, torches to my blindness;
The kolam glimmered white upon the threshold,
The sadam simmered in the pot rich with its milk
And sweetness; I could not see the shivering walls,
The roof that slipped its tiles off like forgotten thoughts,
I could not see the sheets that covered sleeping corpses,
The peerless cloth, spotless, unstained, unspread upon
A marriage bed where still no symbol lay to show
A younger sister's consummation, a virgin's ritual slaying
The crimson unpetalling of her flowering lineage,

Came on her visit, traditional and matriarchal, to see
The children sired by her son; then her throat bore
The weight of heavy golden thali, her nostrils glittered
With its sparkling gem, her toes shining with silver rings
And silk of emerald, verdantly green wrapped regal
Round her frame, her hair parted with proud vermilion,
— her lord now ageing — yet by Death, not unseated
From his throne;
Packed her own food, cooked by her hands, pungent
With curds and spice, tinted with golden glow of saffron
Pooja food for gods, wrapped in its fresh green leaf
So that she should not partake of those hospitable
Yet alien foods from vessels tainted with forbidden
Meats, cooked from the slaughter of those sacred
Avatars that heavenward bore her gods and dreams,
Kamadenu, the milk white cow that carried down to
Earth, Shiva and his consort Parvathi 'earlobes adorned
Ashes smeared from the funeral pyres upon his brow and limbs
Remembering the legends that fed with stories, her children's
Ears, milk that trickling from Parvathi's breast
That fed the hungry Brahmin's child,
A single ritual grain could not be shared
With this new intruder upon whose flesh she looked
Askance, whose blood simmered with exotic jewels
That were unmined from her blood's territories,

30

Flesh that was begotten from those roistering breeds
Who fed on all those unhallowed meats and mated
With those who were not always of their kind,

Daring to share the life that slipped out sacred
From the fortressed domains of her womb, her blood
Spilt at his birth, sacred as the vermilion kum-kum
That streamed upon the bodies of the gods, cleansed
With their oil anointed ritual baths, her blood
Sacrosanct with caste and lineage that never mingled
With that of lesser breed, who sat, not on their threshold
But on those lowly benches set outside their precincts
For mendicants, for wayfarers and wandering swamis,
Holy rishis fed from her hands, for whom she had
Unending compassion — with rice piled high in mounds
Sacred as Mount Meru upon the fresh plucked plantain
Leaf rinsed and warmed pliant by fire, serving
Those holy men their brows painted with Shiva's trident
Their necks weighed down with chains of rudraraksha beads
The dust still thick but sacred from their pilgrimages
On their unwashed feet,

She stood towering beside my bed, flinging her eyeballs
Those frozen stone blue agates like hard boulders to strike
The wounds half healed still festering and bloody on my knife-
Slit, hand stitched body that had given birth, in me, then,
There was no resistance, listened to her words, pronouncements
From her personal vedas —

'I have come,' she said
'I have come only to see
Whether my son is happy,'

Yet slips the golden bracelets on their baby wrists
The manacles of hierarchy, the frail handcuffs to their
Lineage, prisoners that soon would free their lives from
Pinioned cells to fly, or flee, too fine, too brittle, the gold
She brought that later snapped, bits and pieces flung

Into choked up drawers with other emblems, those withering
Twigs of navel chords, which far more precious, nurtured
Them with my rich blood gush from the humus of
My womb, grown from her son's seed, leaving hers
A barren cave, the frozen stalactites sculpted from time
And memory, her mind drowning in ink-black pools
That tunnelled through black bed rock
Cold and subterranean, never reaching light.

It was those others who turned my face
To open windows, women and mothers with auspicious
Wombs, made my gaze alight on fruit hanging on
Branches, heavy and full of sap

'Gaze upon them, feast your eyes on them
Those fruit which will make your breasts
Rich with milk, your blood nourish your children,'
They gently said and boiled those herbs culled
From virgin forests, bunches of leaves rich with
Oil and milk pressing them against my naked flesh
With their strong hands to bring purgation and healing
To those raw wounds, ritual after ritual for my new
Birth, pouring pot after pot of fresh spring water
Heated on the hearth with their surround of raging flames
Until each pore and orifice was catharsized of dross
And I once more, green and fertile as the rainwashed
Earth, stretching once more my arms to sun, to love,

It was not she who showed me kindness
My infants never dandled on her knees,
Her breasts were shrivelled empty of the milk of human
Kindness, yet our hunger leads us to believe
That hands will stretch towards us, lead us to
Those sanctums to nourish those myths the gods
Have taught us to believe;
My husband's love had hope, hope that seduced
My doubts, 'She will welcome you, wash you,
Bath you, comb your hair,' I believed that there

Would be that much kinship to knit in love our
Alien flesh; this could never be.
We were lost, each in our own myths,
Wherein lay naive deception and duplicity.

Now, her hair is white, its parting bare, vermilion
Unstreaked but still she bears her head held high
And wraps the faded silk against her shrunken thighs,
We shared briefly, a span of life, of breath
Baited each other with divergent philosophies
Sometimes poems poured forth from her tongue, she still
Folded hands in prayer. Does she still worship
At a shrine empty of all gods. Is anger lost, to pity?
Arrogance to grief?

The Inheritors

For Norman Simms

Sunshine brilliantly yellow as shed pollen
Shirring the air and the first grapes from
The ancient vine burst out like tiny nipples
Which spurt unvintaged its acrid juice,
Sours a palate jaded with so much nectar
Once youth's ambrosial brew, the sacrificial soma,
God wine of immortality, now the bitter sop
To that unquenched thirst touching the parching
Lips that pucker with distaste in this great
Drought that makes through age, a desert
Of this Canaan land,

Yet, plucks the fruit and sips its wine,
Corrodes the tongue inflamed with burning
Blisters, the delicate taste buds crumple, wither,
With its flame, the mouth, fed with the manna
Of the wilderness, locusts and honey, starves
For that redemptory journey, fed with faith
Into the promised land of that deliverance;

In this country of burnt grass, the heart
Longs for the plump partridge comfort of birds
Rising from the sedges of their water sanctuaries,
Feeding on fish; they are gone, all gone,
Wild duck and pigeon, fields of rosy flamingoes
Migrating to fresher climes and other seasons,
Leaving the eagle, hawk and owl grasping
A quaking mouse, a crow that pecks on carrion,
Bats and flying foxes despoiling mango groves
And ripening orchards, their black limp wings
Clinging like torn wads of hair on yellow-
Eyed branches that open into night;

Wrapped in the leaves of their wet sopping blood
Brought down by gunshot, roasted on death spits
Licked with raging fires, the birds that ride the wind

And clouds have metamorphosed into covey
After covey of fledgelings with the hearts of men,
Stray birds caught in quicklime pits, the thorn
Traps and the snares set by the prowling forest
Hunters, the tangled knots and rope binding
Their trammelled wings,

Here, in the rose garden, there are reminders
Of other deaths, not only the slaughter at the waterhole
But it is death all the same, betrayal in
Our Gethsemanes or temptation in
This new Eden, the living now must move
With those insidious ghosts delicate as faintest
Etchings on transparent blownglass flagons that
Once held wine, flagons that splinter, cracked
By the swinging blow of hurtling stoneglance time;

Wine from these grapes? A finger explores
The light, flicks aside a silvery green leaf
To find the hidden ova clustering like green caviar
That promises a feast where we will view
Those ghosts parading in their stockinette and silk,
Or else, guilt makes us see before us, Banquo's
Ghost, expose the murder in our hearts,
Redden the dusty floor with blood's spilt
Wine from murderous banquets where we feast;

The years have uncellared casques buried
In the cool, dark cobwebbed earth, but its
Breeching from the cave-like grave brings forth
More than these choice banquets, uncorked,
The vapour floats upon the air, clings about
The flaring nostrils, mingles with the pot-pourri
Of ashes, dead as those swollen dreams that make
Our sleep bloat with their longings but then to
Disappear like leeches, shrunk of blood that fall
Off corpses;
Remember our inheritance squandered in

The rose garden, of a family which left its territories
To be redeemed for lucre, a house with two
White pillars and a noble arch, rooms
That we tread, now divest of ghosts, with
Our warm breath drive out mausoleum chill
Stretch our limber shadows on the floor
And walls, move through rooms hushed in
Silence where the sunlight weaves its webs and
White skinned blue-veined hands, ringless and cold
Lie like patient flies, shrouded in folded wings
Readied for the spider death,

Yet, the sunlight beckons, the pomegranates
Ripening hanging like pendulums that strike
And ring the hour, the season's knell, while
The betel vine clings and twines with its cobra
Hooded leaves bringing those ancient legends
Into the garden, but, it is difficult to face
Paradise now or Eden and the blood red thorns
Prickling the green flesh of rose stalks remind
Us that its sting remains embedded in this
Burial place, the humus of the body,
That nothing, not even time can pluck it out
Until the white bone disinters and crumbles
Into dust and we, the ghosts of time walk on
Water, slide through prism bars of light;

We smell the delicate fragrance
Yet do not pluck, allow the flower live just
One hour longer, you tell yourself mortality
Is evident in the petal just about to fall
And the poison scratch of red tipped thorns
Are only too ready to draw blood however
Sluggish its flow within the conduit vein,
The seed that stirs will never be yours again,
Fecundity is dead and lust dry as old leaves
Being mulched into the earth, butterflies stray in
Seeking the nectar that you have finally ceased

To sip and birds peck in the shade arbour
Of the vines at shadows caterpillar soft,

'How like a graveyard' you think as you
Look upon the flower beds dug up with sod
So freshly spread — beneath unbared, the fangs
Of death are tightly clasped about the stone
And root; what dead beast lies with
Its bones crushed, so deep in death, asleep.

Return

Strange chameleon walking on wet pavements
Drenched to the skin rain water
From monsoon rains coursing through
Sandalled toes wet saree folds
Close as tattoos clamped to the body
The smell of frying godambas fills my nostrils
As they flip about my brain like wet white
Sacks flailed by deft fingers of the man
With the sweat soaked banian standing
By the pile of turmeric yellow potatoes
Stuck in soft pyramids in enamel basins
Of the city's eating houses

Food here is a tempting stench that craves
My hunger as I hover like a wheeling fly
Among the loiterers gluttoning on swathed
Turbans of sugary sweetmeats and dazzling
Bangles of jalebis sipping the nectar
Of a pleasure garden

By the entrance to ali mudukku
Stand two prostitutes faces jagged bottle-
Edged, scarred seared puckered remembrance of
Knife wounds on cheeks and arms, slit eyes
Half closed the past screened off under
The scab of lids, purple lips of puffed out
Disintegrating papier-mâché masks,

Slit their minds and find
A million images of copulation
In cobra coils circling about the blurred
Psyches soaked in piss and bile
No one sees the daggers they clutch in
Their hands, the blades that cut out hearts
Like dead wood to throw among the crow shit
And the dung
Their bodies shovelled like shit
Off the paduras each morning

If it ever dawns when the raucous crows
Drum the leaves of the ancient banyan tree in
The wasteland of spent lives
Tossed among rags and old tyres.

They are the dream makers
They sell nightmares by the thousand
If you fish in the black oceans of dementia
With the live bait of your body,
Their trade's not only for cut-throats and thieves
But for respectable citizens who worship
Daily the household gods at domestic shrines
Inheritors of the lineage of lust,

I've come back to the discovery
Of their patois, the insatiable crows
With their black beaks scraping the remains
Of repasts from the banana leaves
And
Dropping coins into palms
As I sit on the seats of tin buses
Or lean my sweat on oil bars of bus stands
Dropping coins as the tambourines flick
With the long nails, scrape nasal twangs,
Hurling tongues of insult in their virudu
At the complacent heads of citizens
Who cower in fear
Pelted by the hard salt
Of their songs.

Blessings that sound like curses
Thud blows on the oiled hair
Scraped back combs into plaits and knots
On heads that know soft pillows and
Bow their heads to all the gods
In obeisance and propitiation

The women in disguise slipping into roles
Bearing framed photographs of family groups

To which they once belonged
Mother, father, children pleading coins
Reminding us of the roles
We dare not discard
Denial, denial of what we truly are

We pray for those beggars imposters
Who are ourselves, the small coin
Of our guilt slips out of heavy purses
The belief in filial love
Respect for elder, family ties
Bonds forged out of the homilies of rituals

No one knows anything about me
Or cares as I walk the streets
A discoloured chameleon, a bedraggled
Fly, jostled by crowds
A lurid Mona Lisa gazing at me
With printed eyes before the heat
Gouges out the colour of their sight
With the quill busily scratching
At my ears, the lens of my eyes
Grabbing picture after picture
That no clock times

The old woman leaning on the stick
And knocking a passage out of the world
As she limps garbles a message
Through her lips
'When I was young
I carried piles of firewood on my head
Chopped logs, baked hoppers night after night
What weights and loads I carried
On my head,
When I was young.'
Now that death is near
Who will bear even a brand to her pyre?

Flight and death at sea

The thunder of the scorched black sea
No more will sound the cries of gulls,
Their throats wrapped round and round
In noose of light tightening the knots
That still their gullets choking in spasms,
Wing swamped, fall, gushed over
With their blood, the salt encrusted feathers
Sharp slice off the spray with razored
Flight and blue sweeps over with its pall
Darkening, to drown, lapping over gaping breast,
Blood and entrails creep out of fleshly cave
Slithering like ruby snail into the azure wave
And wounds are eyes that stare into the sun,
The bullets find the hidden sail, the spray
That tosses high a crest of blood,
The shattered cranium disintegrates
In shells of light, the feathers scatter
As the flesh grows scant, the sea
Peels off the plumes that glittered in the sun,
Blind is the sea to death and lost
Lost the cries of dying gulls.

The poet

The poet must wear uniform
Lose his identity in a cause
Learn a new oath
Share the commonality of a language
Learn to use firearms
Kill! Else, he's a misfit
A laughable object
The mirror in which he once took up
High heroic stance mimics his absurd reflection
Mouths his idiot words
He wears the wrong clothes
His sleeves hang loose
And on the battlefield
Strewn with corpses (of the past)
Waits vainly for miracles and resurrections,
He should be more practical
Rather than expect others to nail him to the cross
He should go into the forest, cut down a tree
Collect his own nails really sharp
Strong ones to go easily through his flesh
So pampered by poesy
Plane his own wood
Set up his cross anywhere
Even in the market place,
Although the people look upon it
As some kind of circus act
Just another gimmick, no longer
A symbol of suffering, where
People are too busy buying and selling
To even take you down
Hail you as their saviour,
Today it's the assassins who are the new messiahs
Their voices herald salvation
With a hail of bullets
And there are others
Whose sufferings have been much greater
Fed the prison food of charcoal and live embers
Their tongues and throats the chalices of bitter wine

Their loose bones shifted out of joint
Now jangle like the keys of cells
That lock us to our prisoned pasts.

Ward 31

Black clay pots demon faces grimacing
In the fields white gaping mouths
Shrieking and swivelling eyes staring up
Rolling and rolling in the zenith of their
Sockets to scare off the greedy birds
That consume the readying harvest

The cries of the sick, white gashes painted
On demon faces conjured out of the dark
Dark folk memory white eyes white lips
The coarse thick lines slashing the leering
Heads, guarding the harvest
Before the grain stalks fall, scythed

Owl-hoots from midnight entrails of pain
Roosting on branches of black skeletal arms
The death auguries of golden eyed birds
As they swoop down tearing through the red
Membranes and clotted fur
Fly back to dark

The skin wraps taut round the bone
Falls slack, gathers up again, mouths
Snarl with black lips puckered up
Drawn back over mask teeth jutting out

Tongues that had cooled on spring waters
Are travelled over with hot flames of fever
And the jungle wood that they bore on their heads
Sparks off, blazes, engulfs and envelops their bodies
In licking fires that consume swiftly
The dry grass of their limbs

The sores are raw inside their guts
Suppurating into the blood and the legs twist
High, thighs raised spread open to Death's
Spectral coition as the poison seeps into them
Twisting in the last rites of orgasm

The skeleton walks in the night, lifting out
Of her grave, eyes stare out and hair knot screwed
Up, her head is the demon pot that tilts
Its grimace at the wild paddy birds
Pecking the ripe grain as they gobble fast
Twisting the stalks in their beaks

Veins dry in the heat and the blood
Is a drought river that the sun has drunk

Coughs gulf through in spasms of thick phlegm
Women hunch over creep back foetal into wombs
Of pain gestate themselves pushing tears and gasping
Breath into their unclenching palms

She lies there feet hands knotted up
Tied to her bed, the terror of her cries
Clamped over as she shakes
Frenzied and her brain skewered on a spit
Cooking over the raging flames of her madness
To feed the demons that tear her sinewy flesh

Old women tearing open their bodices,
Gasping for air
Thrust out their dishevelled cries

We are all travelling through endless forests
Of pain, routless paths and the darkness of leaves
And trees lurch into your body, footfall
Knocking against stone hearing the rustle of
The death serpents under the scrolls of ferns
The jungle ticks fastening into your flesh
Hopping off the wounded beasts
As they follow the bloodied spoor.

We are flung together grainless sacks
That have fed the famished mouths
We are the spent granaries the empty

Paddy bissa now hollow for the snakes
To creep, gourds that are shrivelled dry
Hard skinned with fever's heat
In the dying chenas

Vomit gushes out of my guts
Floods the floor spreads out
A map of my sickness an island of bile
Touches the mat of the sleeping woman
Under my bed, I ask for a sip of water
There is no cup, I delve back into the rivers
Of my dreams, find I swim in a blood streaked
Spume that lifts from the current,
Taste on my cracked lips
Its bitter spittle.

The garden

There's no forecast of my life
    among the long spread shadows
    of the garden   the hours I spend here
    are a life-time
    watching the sun's posturings
    on a wing on a lizard's
    scale   on this leaf
    of earth
    water branches into air
    skyways the birds
    flight at cross roads
    of the clouds
    to pass my life
    left behind
    a mountain's stance
        my head buried beneath
        the roots I drink rain

Birdsongs are fences
    within my wild
    roving orchards shelter,
    fruit scatter their burst
    wounded flesh

Quake heart or be fearless
    you too
    you too are not here
    long to stay

There's no forecast of my life
    among the long spread shadows
    of the garden   yet
    the hours I spend here
    are a lifetime
        my head buried beneath
        the roots I drink rain.

Beneath the snow

It is on these rainy nights I remember
When dark like an earwig crawls in
To seek the dry of listening ear
Then the dream returns through wind
Wrapped like wet hair swathes
Coiling and coiling round and round
My mind, glistening strands sparkling with
Moisture and fragrant with the Queen of the Night
That grows by my window

When your face lies on my palm
Cupped memory and I stroke it softly
Moulding and moulding it, crystal gazing
Into your eyes is now a no future from a present
That was so quickly becoming a past

At the same time the bombs in Dionysiac
Rage make a welter of limbs spurting with
Their wine blood out of the burst goat skins
Of flesh to splurge the pavements of our lives
Those of us who escaped take henna patterns
Of blood decorating the soles of our feet,
The palms of our hands painted with death flower
Petals that have a different fragrance,
We are the brides of death
Widowed so early in our grief

There, the flowers breathed beneath the snow
The ice fragrance of no colour buried beneath
A hard earth and the winter flakes fell
As we stood at the window looking out on a changing
View turning your cheek from darkness to light
From season to season towards a spring
We would never share or never know

Puberty rites

'You are now a big girl,' they said
'You have attained age'
The taboo period of seclusion over with ceremonies
Pots of water poured over my head by the reddi nenda
Who came from Deiyangewella — the field of the gods —
She of the ruddy skin and long silver-pierced ear lobes
The white towel scrubbed on stone
Thrown over her shoulder
She who ironed our clothes, the hot iron
Spitting out its heat with the sprinkled moisture
Pressing the stiff starch into crackling folds
Puffing out gathers, folding the smell of sun
And water into white school uniforms
Pleating our seasons into orderly growing
Arm lengths of sheets squared and folded into shape
The stains of our lives bleached out of Irish linen
Spread on sunned grass and stone to crackle dry,
The iron filled with smouldering coconut shell
Embers taken from the burning hearth

Reddi nenda who brought carved brass bandesi
Of rasa kaveli for the Aluth Avuruddha
Covered with pure snow-white embroidered cloths
Edged with tatting renda, piled with
China plates of Kewun ekled into honey
Crumbling kondé palm flat atirasa and
Saffron yellow kokies, finger-pressed seeni
Kema thick crystal with sugar syrup and
Asmi streaked with pani,
    Diamond shapes of aluwa and kiribath
    Moulded flowers embedded in the milk
    Rich grains, the comb of plantains
    Painted with white chunam for ripening
She whose hands were red knuckled
With steeping dirty clothes in rivers and streams
She who always smelt of sun and water
Soap and sago starch, carrying on her head
Neatly combed, oiled, the knotted bundle

Of washed clothes across the railway track
One hand steadying as her narrow hips swung
Her neck arched into taut muscle-stretched straightness

Poured pot after pot of water on my head
In ritual cleansing of the strains that new dreams
Left from wet leaves that brushed and clung
To my new breasts from the thick knit forest of dark
From the fruit that ripened, split, bared
Its teeth, bit into flesh
My long hair swathed with water
Her hands soothing the turmoil
Of weltering waves now dipped with
The richness of irrigated fields
Streaming with rivulets, the earth now silver,
And then her two hands
Twisted with silver bangles lifting
Broke the pot at my shattered feet.
'Now you are no longer podi-bebi
Now we will call you missy
When you marry you will be called nona.'

Days bound in white napkins
As blood sped from my body

'She has grown up' they said with love
And pride, relatives made gifts encircling
My fingers with family heirlooms
Golden rings studded with topaz, zircon, aquamarine
Telling me that I was now ready
For love and procreation

The pieces of shattered pot gathered up
Flung no one knows where
The water flowed away
From the body like cut vein

Red the drooping cockscombs
Of the slaughtered bird that screamed
At dawn
Red the simmering ants that crawled
On the nectar of the spoiled jak fruit fallen
Red the bee stabbed hibiscus
Red the blood of my new wounds

Repetition of rituals
For my daughters whose bodies
Tremble with the cold of splashing water
Bright the gold on their wrists
Bangles taken from mine
My hands cut in diamond shapes
Legends and myths from the platters
Of milk rice to feed dreams to each other

Falling into the river the full moon
Bleeds slashed by the blazing chulu
Lights of the night-fishers.

His family

I fight ragingly against the representations
Of their society, their figures
Etched on the skyline
Huddling like crows with purple beaks
Dipped in blood and carrion flesh
Whom they must yet appease
With food blessed upon their plates

Theirs is an empty society
Torn up from weakening roots
'Tradition,' they tell me 'was strong once,
In our village, men stepped aside on roads
Unwinding their shawls, at our approach
And wealth we had, elephants, palanquins, lands,
The banknotes taken from locked safes
Rinsed out in light were laid out to dry
On mats spead out in the ul-muttham,'
Golden sovereigns clinked, sifting through
Jewelled fingers
The koel's cry was then auspicious
Heralding the renewal of each birth cycle,
After marriages were arranged
According to caste and horoscope

Goat heads dripping blood from velvi rituals
Brought into the kitchens, gash marks set like
Reddest rubies in their necks, fingers
Daubed with blood stains like kum-kumum
Of Kali's rituals, went into the simmering cooking pots,
He died young that grandfather partaker of those banquets
Leaving a daughter sickened with so much voluptuousness

Now ghosts ride the phantom palanquins
And the elephants long ago shed their ivory
Two were left, set in carved ebony
Probably sold by an exigent brother
Or looted by the mobs

They stood, then, at the head of Pata's coffin
And he laid out in ivory silk draped
In shawl bordered with crimson and gold
We, his daughters-in-law had looted
The wealth of his loins, stood now
With our children scattering coins
On his wasted flesh

In archives lie the sannasas of the past
Cherished by history, guarded from silverfish
Crumbling to the touch disintegrating in our fingers
Like buried skin, no one to decipher
An ancient script, only rumours, rumours
And recollections vague, fading of myths,
Tributes and Capture, gifts of groves and fields
Where now the mines are laid
Blasting hierarchy along their way
Scattering in shreds each fleshly page

The house recedes and the walls
Delve down into their own burial
Encountering emptiness
They leave no heirs to defend this last inheritance

Holed in within cracked tombs
Hidden behind the sandbags and the battered walls
Lie the sons of a different ancestry
Bridegrooms of death
That await the final consummation
There's fire in the streets
For the agni worshippers
They tread on ash
No sacred yaham's left
For them, garlanded, three times to circumambulate
The bullets chant the vedas

53

And the bows of epic heroes
Arc in the curving hand
Of a flung grenade
The sons of this family
Do not ride the chariots to battle
In these new mythologies

We see each other

We see each other in our new nakedness
She, now stripped of silk and gold
And I with merciless eyes
No longer blind to myths,
Her body that once was bathed in milk
Laved with jewels — cold stones that
Gathered heat from each her breasts
And sparked off fire before each brilliant
Dulled and flickered to end its death
In fall of ashes

Swathed in crimson readied for the bridal
Chamber at sixteen
'The nautch girls came and put the flowers
In my hair, the jewels they adorned me with,'
Her small body held much dower
Her territories wide, her fields were rich
Now juts a crooked hip out like disjointed wing
Bright feathers with their youth and sheen
Plucked off to leave her body bare and chill
Stripped quills that dipped in lineaged blood
Once wrote their histories
In gestation of their kind

Breeding willed, fertility a social rite
And first denied, or so she thought, by gods
Of children, followed her society's decrees
Went on pilgrimages, poured milk upon the stone
And wrapped the garlands culled from her own prayers
About the Shiva lingam piled round with fruit
And warmed with fire, to breathe desire and life
Into her new lord's limbs

Where love had not thought fit to shape her life
For procreation, beseeched all Kailasa's deities
To make the seed spring fecund in her barren womb
And make a pooja of the act of consummation
Emptying from her clasped hands, offerings
Of fulsome fruit and budding flower that spelt fertility

Now drank the nectar of its juice
Where earlier love had only left a bitter savour
Now brought forth through her faith
Both sons and daughters
Made of love's act, to please the gods
This new penance in guilt's expiation

Who knows what shaped her dream
Of karmic birth her dead brother
To become re-incarnate as her progeny
Found in those supernatural night journeyings,
From another world wrapped in a groaning haze
Of red and swirling dust, drawn down
Down into the netted hammock

Swinging on mind trees
Into her psychèd womb
From where she pushed him forth
Impelled by that incestuous love
Which gratified her groping search
Creating flesh of her flesh blood of her blood
While yet another sprouted from the seed
Just as she had let the other out

Her fields were rich, ploughed by the gods
Its earth now veined with gold
The gods sent rains, no drought assailed
Those harvests, the sheaves so richly garnered
Filled her plenteous store with mound of grain
Bursting with milky kernel

She talked to gods
Prayed at her household shrine
Lit lamps until her fingers burnt
Like oil soaked wicks
That blazed their fire-licked brands
To light those pyres
She stood afar and did not watch them burn
Rubbed on her forehead ash whitening her brow
Taken, until they emptied
From the urns of memory.

Still life

Those great Dutch paintings of still life
In Van Dyke's museums of death
Canvasses heavy with fruit and flowers
Trussed game, dead hare, shot pheasants
And gaping fish but death made pleasantly
Beautiful, a purloinment of life, you look
Not so much at wounds as the markings so perfectly
Brushstroked into feather fur or fin
The blood drops from death-parched tongues
Already dry with the paint to endure for centuries
Flowers that never lose colour, never wither
Nurtured by the eternal plasma
Of the past's lifegiving blood.

Let us paint the new still life and let the
Painters be anonymous taken from the street
Or beach or some remote hamlet

The game brought in fresh from the forests
With still steaming flanks and pant half
Felt as the breast heaves thirsting for
Great gulps of death

To arrange the carnage of limbs
Round deathflowers, tongues lolling
Out or swallowed whole choking with the rush
From bursting blood aqueducts
Or between purpling beaks
Squashed up spurting fruit
Fingers plucked off, red gold pistils
And stamens crushed obscene rites
In pornographic deathshots
Ivory flesh splattered on black
Regaled with seething mantles and cloaks
Silkening flowing in crimson from each
Erupting gash

With careful fingers arrange the stalks exuding

57

A resin of blood stuck into matted fur pads,
The eyes of snared shot game, glazed, do not
Reflect the shadow of the natural flower, the thick
Pollen droppings, scattering gold tears onto fringed
Fins that droop, now lost the flutter of
Ocean windshawls on tremulous shoulders
Of frothing water

We do not see the hunter
Washing the bloodstains off his hands
Or smell the burnt flesh on singed hair
Where the bullet went in.

The fish struggles inside you, a dying
Heart that heaves as the hook guts in

We see the perfect picture
the aureole of flowers and a life-like bee
Stinging out nectar
We do not smell the rotting stalks
Wrenched from roots in crystal vases
Crudded with staling water oozing
Malignant fluids out of fibres and flesh shreds
Nor do we smell its decomposition
Or touch the softening body bulging with old
Blood as the sunshafts pierce through the glass
Windows;
Not on our fleshsmocks
The splashed blood splotch, on the
Palettes of our hands, crimson

Let us set fire then to the masterpieces
And efface the museums
Which show
A flower as only a flower
A fruit as fruit
Where only the dead game tells us
That once there was life.

Chatsworth I

The mirror reflects our fictions as we build
Image after image and event after event
Into the architectures of our visions

Nobody seems to be alive here
Only the ceilings surge with a seventeenth century
Christ in a heaven envisioned by Laguerre,
The prayers in the family chapel were formal
The priest addressed Christ in a period tongue
They knelt in hierarchic prayer,
Here, there was no stuff of martyrs
No one wore hairshirts

And gardens cascade with gradients of water
And the spume of fountains
Rise and fall, vague hands sweeping away
The miasma of the trimmed and ordered landscape
Yet the wraiths of history
Still skulk in the gazebos and ornate pavilions,
Arrest the intruder

How can anyone forgive such voyeurism,
Peering into and through mirrors
We pause,
Surmise and ponder on the amours
Of the dead, startle ghosts who watch and wait
Biding their time until they too are joined
By the newly dead

It is only the paintings that are alive
Here, each enactment continues
Within a frame
Napoleon standing on a barren isle,
Europa raped.

Derbyshire, 8th October 1985

59

Chatsworth II

There is not a single fly that buzzes
Against the window pane nor ant creeping
Through narrow channels of light that flow in
From cloud arboured skies, yet the air is full
Of their breathing, they must be somewhere here
Watching me, watching you, disturbed at our
Human smell,

Even in their sleep they must hear the tramp
Of feet up and down the stairways along the
Passages and corridors, startled,
Awake to find a stranger's eyes alight
Upon a slender ghost that vanishes,
Now less substantial than a wraith of thought
That yet leaves behind upon the marble
Malachite or chinoiseries, a strand
Of hair, a thread of gold to be reminder
Of that other life that dwelt in private worlds
Closed to these surging crowds

You reach to touch and feel but it deceives
A trompe-l'œil of time, that violin
Of burnished wood, taut strings and arching bow
No hand can touch, no arm lift down to play
Those haunting airs gavottes, and minuettes and sarabands
For silken feet that sweep the floor

Carved mythic animals press their clawed feet
Into a plush of velvet pile, the gilded chairs
Embrace the ghostly fragrance of those perfumed shoulders
While attar of roses, pot-pourris of flowers
Cling like dust and ashes in the glazed tombs
Of urns and jars

Wine tips into those cavernous throats
Dry with the heat of memory's thirst
Flowing through alabaster with its crimsoned vein
They have all arisen with their lovers,

Left their beds and chairs to join with shades
Drift slowly past like dusty motes in sunlight
That beams those feeble rays to fall on us, intruders
As we pass through the private galleries
Of unknown lives and visored faces.

Derbyshire, 8th October 1985

The death carvers

We talk as if it is another country
The harsh rock of flesh hacked with hatchets
The secret men with masks who belong to bloodnights
The death carvers, but no blade is delicate enough
To chisel something that gives like moss
What adheres can be scraped off with fingernails

Someone has to wipe the blades clean
Remove the smell of old blood

Does the flesh cry out at this impingement
The long cuts gape to show the hard bone
The singing sinews that twang with mourning
Voices before the strings give?

On the face of the sky a grimace of stars
The moonlight congeals like fat
Splattered over with darkening gouts
On bodies lifted with their wounds
Vanishing into the forest,
Into night.

OM

The experience
        Is reiterated statement
        Travelling through the cerebral passage
        To reveal new insights
Complexities fall apart
        Leaving the vertebrate clean of flesh
        Its white bone feathers
        Quill pointed in the sand
        Through the temple door's eye —
        Dark slit
                The day is a turquoise wave
                Bisected by a seagull wing
Where I stand
                — Stepping out of sunwaves

        Drowning in this molten heat —
        Lies the samadhi of a saint
        Swept by shore winds
        The sands encroach
        On his endless meditation
        Pressing silence upon silence
        At the abandoned altar
        Stripped of its ritual
        We search for a lost dialect
        And speak to gods
        Out of our own silence
        Gazing into the darker solitude
        Of Siva's eyes, we discover
        The reincarnate desires of our personnae

The peacock lamps
        Tongue flickering flame snuffed out
        The last breath of camphor
        Impregnates the coral walls
        And through the listening ear
        Quiet to its own thought
        The nearing sea whispers

Its continuing syllable
    OM,
Through the convolute echoes
Of oncoming night.

Numerals

We now explore new obsessions
With explosions reverberating in our ears
We keep secret diaries in our minds
Times dates numbers events
We take long ropes knot them
Sliding our hands over protuberances
Unravel the length and wind it once
Again around and round the tethered neck
Notch trunks of trees before they become
The gallows stakes or pyres
Carve out cells in the brain
Brim them with the scarlet shrouded
Corpses killed in a plague of war

Today a hundred and fifty shot
Yesterday seventy blasted
Even the poet becomes numerate
The preoccupation is not only with words
The metaphor becomes a bullet ridden numeral
Militants killed in a shoot out
Three killed in ambush
The map erupts with gigantic bubbles of blood
Bursting and flooding the lacerated terrain
Columns of figures, hundreds and thousands
Swept away by the inundation of the flood

Does anyone record the graphs
Of dwindling pulse, hold a mirror
To the dying breath, still the spasms
Of the wounded breast?
What else is there to contemplate
But death?
The tokonomas, murals, frescoes, grafitti
Bear sketches scrawls paintings of
grinning gargoyles, Deaths Heads, spectres
Of the battlefields

Among the sibilant fountains
Jetting blood in parks and gardens
We take our fearful walks
Skulking in mazes or emerge
Among trampled flowerbeds
And are reminded of the trenches
Which the victims dig, shot at from behind
They tumble into

The battle escalates
Now no one talks of peace
The meditation of the sages hid away
In their caves is interrupted by
The sound of gunfire
As the echo ceases and the hills draw nearer

Horror is the deadly nightshade

Horror is the deadly nightshade
In my mind that blooms with dark
Within its throat I lie impaled
Before I drown and die
Sucked in within the viscous fluid
Of its guts

Poison floods my being as I gasp
Knocking against each insect corpse
That dangles from its gibbet sides
Petals rasp against the skin, dehydrate
Now of sap.

In that garden grew both flower and fern
Embowered in the greenest moss
Yet there the bee still stabs the firmest bud
With shaft of greed, from its embrasure
Levels death and butterflies
For all their colour and their sheen
Drenched in that heady nectar
Fall wrapped in shrouds of pollened death.

Caravaggio

The bare canvas of the cell
Waits for its subject to arrive
The table's spread for supper, the last,
The bread and wine laid out
The tilting chalice lifted by a faltering
Hand to spill and stain
The spotless napery that wipes
Those frothing lips to splotch with red
Immaculate white

Repetitious enactments of those rituals
Waking our sleeping senses to new
Revelations that beam their light
To score the fruit of blindness deeply,
Wound the grape and scythe the harvest
For its bloodied grain,
Feed our constant hungers
Appease our lust for pain

Arrange his body, posture his limbs
Let your brush abrade, contuse the naked
Flesh and draw the nail marks
Of its patterned bruises on his body's cross,
Make of his torturers, the Caravaggios
Of our time,

The still life comes alive
Walks to his tongue
Beseeches teeth to bite into his crust
The chalice is replenished fills and brims,
The postulant imbibes its heady liquor
Then vomits out its yellow bile

His head swoons, drowned in thornéd waves
Of his delirium dreams, dark obsessions
Screech, the vultures of his sleep,
Knives crash stone through and splinter
Glassy flesh, dementia crawls, the sated

Maggot of heretical thought
Feeds with greed upon the carrion of his brain

His body's sodden crust falls
Into your cupped palm; its morsels
Hold; receive his agony, eat, drink
That you may share what he so freely gave,
Bow your head, feel resurrection stir
Within your body's tomb, the miracle here,
Lies in the cavernous emptiness, the raided
Sepulchre a necessary fact, now that the stone
Is rolled away, to re-affirm, restore,
A lost and broken faith.

Glasgow

It is as if the streets have lost
Their way and reach nowhere, signs of
Inns and pubs neon-lit hotels
Bed and breakfast joints have fallen
Off so that the promised shelters
Are never there, the comfort long felt
And now desired of sheets, wrapping round
Jammed limbs and the heat of rooms
Closed to winter's winds will never again
Promise to whip up blazes in the blood
There is no dream of woods in spring
To lie in, pollen from golden flowers
Dusting into nostrils and tulips slowly
Bleeding from staunchless wounds, opening
The arteries of the season, day after day
To feed new blood into our sluggish veins

I have lost my way, the traffic lights
Gone blind allow for violent collisions
One runs up against danger here, anywhere,
The casual encounters turn lethal and the
Armclasp hostile turns into a throat strangle
Flight tilts you into the deep drains
Of the city, even as you emerge from the glittering
Theatres with arias ringing in your ears
Voices pouring like decanted wine from crystal
The sewer rats bloat in the darkness
And the old men scrabble in the bins
Hold out their caps for pence, slash open the cans
To swill their beer, their laughter and ribaldry
Echoes from dark corners, the old lady with
Raddled cheeks and bright red lips
Haunts the liquor shop, stands on the pavement
Ranting at invisible phantoms that jostle her
Accosts me 'I'm hungry' she complains,
'Give me money for a bag of chips,'
The bibulous drinkers from the bars
Crowd in the shining mirrors

In which, all perspectives lost,
There is no distance

Our flat shadows walk on flat plains
Our eyes white with snow
We fall, grope with blunt claws
Touch the shape of carrion
Feel ice at the lips, chill creeping
Into the throat, freeze, our souls
Perish, we are buried, consciously
Under sweeping drifts

In the frozen pond birds skate
On ice-islands floating
Indifferent past, our wraiths

The stubborn image

We are constantly confronting the stubborn image
The one in the mirror turned inwards into flesh
That refuses to change — not accept the distortion
Twisting the mouth with wry lips that utter lies
The treacherous kisses, peeled off like rind
From the worm eaten fruit
The throat choked with the poisoned juice
That wells the tongue
To brim with tasting Death,
Our ears splintered with bone words
Pierce into the nerves to deafen first
The thunderclap of wakening, then meet silence
Turned to stone or imprisoned, insect-like in amber.

Looking into mirrors we choose the image
That stays with the dream, virginal, pure
Uncorrupt, illusion's naive bride as if
No contagion has ever touched the screen
Of silver flesh, no pustulent sore that bursts
Oozes and spreads a plague of lust
That speaks of ravished death

Death in the afternoon

Death in the garden
Under the trees with the flowers
Blooming, perhaps a bird or two
Moving startled on the branches
New flowers bloom crimson, scarlet, red
Fallen on the green grass, death in the
Afternoon in the midst of singing, in the
Heart of silence,
Death stalks where silence falls
And feline springs, ferocious,
People listening sitting under the trees
Hear fireworks splutter,
    Not so, guns upraised shoot,
    The sun bleeds, the flowers scattered
    It's death in the afternoon

Boats

The boats are full of the dead
Bobbing gently over the waves
The shark sun drinks their blood
That floats in finning trails,
Under the skin the bones jut out
Where the wind flails
Their hand clutched the dew
To draw it to their lips
Taste raw the blood from blistering skin,
Night voyage begins
Night that for us is scent of
Flower or moon or lovers
Clambering out of sleep
Night for them is death.

Snares

Right to the bitter end that much
No more the fall into the camouflaged
Pits that snare with spike and thorn
To settle there crippled and with broken
Limb until the stake tears shredding
Into heart
    It's in the forest that I lose my way
I knew my path would lead beyond the arid
Water hole to yet some trackless way
Ignore all warning signs and sounds
The broken twig downfallen trees
Slashed branch shed leaf and scattering
Fruit torn from their stalk by squawking
Bird
    But all around me silent beasts
Safe in their lairs or stalking prey

We search our death as life we've known
Too long, safety we leave and stop our pulsing time
As clocks that drop their hands
And tell us that our sleep is near
All time elapsed

    And night is here.

Assessment of failure

I am reminded now reaching the twilight
Of my age, no longer looking forward
To any kind of peace since that would be
Both decadent and illusionist
In a world once thought deceptively Utopian

I am reminded in this half light
Made lurid by the great wounded sun
Raging downhill like maddened boar
Through a grassland of flames
Tushed wounds gaping wide
Rushing headlong into the piled carcasses
Strewn far and wide, rooting up
Hefty chunks of earth, goring into
And encountering stumps of limbs and
Bodies burnt and cut, the flesh still smoking,
The genitalia charred and black wads of hair
Crumbling into grey-white ash

I am reminded of
My days of youthfulness, a student
Walled in within those newly hallowed
Walls of learning, imbibing savour after savour
From the trash heap of alien traditions
Or perched in an ivory tower
Waiting like Danae for that golden shower,
Descent occasional to blindly tread Parnassian
Paths in Pastoral landscapes where those antique
Shepherds led their bleating flocks to pasture
Cropping a Roman Summer's tender grass
Before it turned in hardening earth
To winter stubble

Walking in orchards or plucking grapes
In vineyards not yet cratered by bombs
Or sprayed by bullets,
We tasted wine, we tasted wine
Twisting our contorted limbs

In Bacchanalian dance, read erotica
Translating words into words, not acts
Of the Satyricon of Petronius Arbiter

My eyes flew out of windows
Onto flowering trees past the white pages
Lying unread before me, rubbing a haze
Of pollen over a dreaming vision unaware
That my body was ready for pleasure
Toying with lines of poetry, peering into mirrors
A floating image of a body's barque
Drifts into darkness caught in those dallying
Hours to vanish in those reeded shallows

Sitting under a shaded light
Focussing a pool of brightness
On a map of Caesar's conquests
Translating line after line scraped off
Like fungus on a mouldering, dead
Catacombed tongue, translating strategies
Of battles into a language not my own
From a language not my own
Of events in a country not my own
Of wars and invasions, unaware of parallels
Unable to trace routes, make connections
With those histories that belonged to a past
In which I had no stake, no share
Recreating an in memoriam of De Bello Gallico

Death at sea

The boat swings on the waves and the voices
Of children cry with the sea-gulls swooping
Over the sails, fish breathe beneath green
Water, quivers the slightest shape of silver
Glinting to sport and leap into
Sunlight as if arching fin sprouts
Wings cleaving to trees of waves
Sliding through water branches,
Froth breathes through spume
Showers in shocks of tendrilling
Foam lifting and spreading in
Finest spray, through the warm
Currents the shoals travel
The sharks are hidden
The horizon clear
Over the luminous scarab of the sea
Sunlight now silver, scrawls
The lucid messages of day
The blue eye of death
Closed against the dazzle winks
Out the blinding darkness that
Leaps like silver blade to
Dismember ripple or surging wave

The boat swings and smoothly heaves
Through the beginning passage of the straits
Who knows that soon the slaughter
Will begin, knives at the waist spring out
To slash and chop limb from limb as
They struggle, each their bodies against
A closing net of steel, choke at the gill,
One spasm two or three leap and then lie still
Quick quick and deft they wield the knives
No swerve of blade to halt the killing
Ungutted now, lie to spoil, fins crumple
With the weight of blood, scales grow dull
Peeled off their colour and their shine
Dull eyes glazed filmed over, covered

With its pall blackens at the edge
Of severed flesh

Yet, see how gently the boat swings
And the fish still travel through
The passage of the sun before the moon's
Strong tides draw them back into the darkening chill

The gulls with white and peerless breast
Swoop over the crimsoning waves
The vast seas reddening honeycomb
Breaks, dripping swarms with
Hidden corpses thick fed with the
Crimson pollen of their death
The bitter nectar seeps into the wave
Is borne away, where the silver fishes
Netted in a mist of spray still
Still in the sunlight glide and leap

Murals of violence

The myths must be translatable in our times
Mind mould in gigantic bas-reliefs
The death feasts, both host and guest
Monstrous in their debauchery, slavering
Over the carnage, an heroic dream of epic
Turning into nightmare Colossus
Roves upon the planet orbed with flames
Charring the sticks of bones piling up
Upon the shores while stalking through
The skeletal tumuli gigantic beasts
Horns antlered to the sky, wreathed
With victorious death skulls cloven
Hooved, hides thick with clotted fur
Stampede upon the battlegrounds;
The reek of meats from the banqueting
Halls, the tables heaped with steaming
Platters of flesh, wreathe round the walls
And pillars, the choking miasma of their
Breath, the bestial appetites of war
Fed on each massacre
Whetted with fresh hunger for more
And more of battered flesh
Torn apart with ravening fangs
Slaver and slop over the brimming
Dishes of the feast, gorging themselves
Upon the swelling fruit crowded with
Maggots from the festering honey
Of the grave, or plucked with bloodied
Hands from the orchards of the underworld,
The carcass of the doomed, the hanged
And tortured blistered with gunshot
Scored with blades of steel, seared
With flames and roasted on the spits of hell
Now set upon the platters of the feast
Carved with great knives of hate
Flagons of bitter wine, empty more
And more, until the senses reeling
Deep in their cups, engorged and

80

Bibulous the banqueters, sprawl and snore
So long they have battened on the dead
Their veins corrode with poison
They strew the devastated earth
With bones picked clean of flesh
But now lie weak as flies
Settling on the remnants of the feast
Perishing in a plague of war

A question of identity

The talk comes up
In odd places
Who are you?
What are you?
Are these all mirror questions
Reflections of interior conflict and dissension
Or do we answer under some compulsion
When you face the interrogators
In the streets and public places
When the hunt is up
And the bloodhounds bay at you
Deathsquad after deathsquad
In full outcry scenting strange blood
The odour of fear gives you away.

I examine my bones
The structure of the anthill
With its teeming mazes
And find within another race
Toiling away at its new usurpation
We travel counter but emerge
At the same point, we share a destination.

It wasn't important before
Questions like 'Who were the Nazis?'
'What did they do?' took precedence
In classroom, lecture hall, salon,
We sat in judgement eyewitnessing history
By proxy, the Rise and Fall of Empires
The decline of power and morals
The decadence and licentiousness of society,
Were the subjects of our theses
Steeped in the historicity of alien civilizations.

We carefully explained, the footnotes coloured
With rhetoric, the illustrations copious —
That extermination was the past time
Of other races perpetuating each their own myth,

And page after page in the history books
Had nothing to do with you or me,
We were innocent, guilty neither of conspiracy nor sedition
Led our ordinary lives, went to market, rocked babies
In cradles, shot game enjoyed our blood sports
Put the animal out of its agony like gentlemen
Captured butterflies, waltzed in crowded ballrooms
Never featured in the headlines
We were merely onlookers, observers, history's rapporteurs.

Content with the green sward of our territory
As yet unmined, we were innocent of genocide
Or warmongering, our sins were venal
It was easy at the confessional to seek absolution
We had hope at least of salvation in another life
Prayed for mercy, received forgiveness,
The horror had no documentation in our chronicles
And epics, the ancient heroes were our gods
We renewed the garlands at their anniversaries
Placed wreaths at their altars, the smoke of incense
Was not then of carnage — the fires were for purgation
There were no new heroes to take their place
The proselytised saved had no need of armaments
Seeking another kingdom, the meek and humble
Were promised a different inheritance
We bowed our head to sword and hatchet
As if it were a new dispensation
But later, we too were to have
Our autos-da-fé, those who did not recant
Went up in flames.

Partisanship, alliances where they existed
Were biased, we sided with the conquerors
Fought against those who were not our enemies
We, the subjugated clapped our hands at their victories
Wept at their defeat, applauded the triumphal entries
Into vanquished cities, in our ears rumbled
The armoured cars and tanks

Sweeping over the bombed ruins
Bodies slowly suffocated beneath the rubble
Unretrieved, time would yield their bones
Relics of wars ossuaries.

We found justification for their sabotage and resistance
Considered invasion a vindication of honour
Our analyses of history were interpolations
Of partiality, we crowned heroes — they were
Not our own — with laurel wreaths
We were the campfollowers to the victors
Caught the bullets and sabre thrusts in our breasts
Were buried in Flanders, El-Alamein, Dunkirk
Plunged burning into cities and seas of ice
Where the fires were frozen

They died with honour for a cause
We were yet to find, war and violence
Battlefields and death belonged so we thought
To the holocausts of other nations,
The mass of rubble splattered with blood
Men blown up, hands tied behind their backs
Children and old people shot at from point blank range
Death in the sanctuaries are now part
Of our own history and we, the guilty, its perpetrators

The question is 'Why did they come?'
Motives? I never questioned them before
Between the facts and the dates
The portraits and the clever cartoons
Lies the clue to an identity

It belonged within one of those eras
Maps show clearly the routes
Posterity carried the genes on to another
One had Dutch forebears and a great-grandmother
Who spoke Portuguese, an easy patois

Left behind by the conquered
Others were proselytised in church or Audience Hall,
Their coffers brimmed, coffee gardens flourished
Or were blighted, their easy philanthropy left us
Bereft and orphaned; their dress and manners
Foreign to this clime, their language, as an era
Changed now that of the conqueror,
In their hands they bore Bibles and gold
Commodities of trade, progeny for their lives
Continuance, fire arms for preservation,
It is only now that identity becomes important
We do not wait for Judgement Day to open graves
We rift through tombstones, archives, searching names
Find connections that are not mere forgeries of blood.

The buzzing hive was vitiated with corruption
The drones apathetic the queen bee heavy with
Infertile eggs, lethargic, the honey gatherers worn out
The pollen rusty, the bitter honey growing out of mould
The hissing snake lay close to the hive
The leeches avid for bloodsucking
Carrion collection over the harvest of battlefields
Sunshafts damp with mist seeped
Into gouged out eye sockets blood spilt
Lay sharp on the stone congealing and clotting
From the wounds of dead men and dead horses.

The talk comes up
When I want to be separate
When I have to defend myself against
The conservative morals of other tribal groups
The question of identity,
We share the same guilt
We were once invaders
Whether Commandant, predikanten
Conquistador or Koopman
On our brows eating into skull
We bear branded the mark of Cain.

I have no country

I have no country now but self
I mark my boundaries extend demesnes
Even beyond the darkness of those regions
Still to be explored, chart my ocean voyages
In blood or stay becalmed watching a gull
Impale its shadow on a thorn of wave.
Waiting for the winds to blow to set once more
In motion the pattern of the sea, a ripple stir
Into a wave that sweeps, tidal, wide horizons,
Rises above a cloud to drench the sky
And pours its deluge on the stars to drown
All lights and in that darkness find again
New brightness from a self created firmament
The cosmic mind imagines, to choose one star
Out of a galaxy or constellation, constant as
The Pole's unmoving light whose spokes glittered
On the waves to guide through an unknown and
Blinding dark, the voyages of ancient mariners
Through oceans to reach those lands as yet unmapped
And undiscovered.

Once more to journey on a chartered course
To reach which country? One that I must know
Before this birth or one that others more intrepid
Had discovered so that for me there's no new
Adventure left and nothing new for exploration
Except the landmarks racing through my blood
Or found in ruined fortresses and artefacts
In archives and in museums.

What subterfuge of islands draw me near
Destruction, here, snares already set, the pit is staked
With poisoned thorns and ragged branches,
My footsteps trapped with guile, I fell headlong
Through the camouflage, the hunt made easy
For both hunter and for poacher. And remain
My gait now fractured, couched on a bed of thorns
Wait for what death will come, through knife or bullet.

This was perhaps my choice. So I stay here
Iconoclastic of all statues, images
Covering the walls of sacred places,
The saints too good, too pure and too unreal
To be my guides although they too follow paths
That can only spell new dangers.
Heretical my thought and that of all unbelievers
Yet out of a loss of faith
For our salvation, we seek once more
A stronger faith; my fear is that escape
From martyrdom makes our complexion and
Our stature, coward. Cowering for safety
In the camps to which we flee for refuge
And remain with other fugitives who have escaped
From fire and slaughter for all time disinherited.

Interrogation

Guilt is never one's own
It is always that of others
Innocence can be proved coercively
If the truth's repudiated
Make even the cassock cringe.

We are not sentimental about priests
We know that they are all too human,
Divinity does not lie
In the fabric of a garment
It is the vulnerability of nakedness
We explore, we who are not
The interrogated, but someday, sometime
We will find ourselves
At the mercy, absolute, of someone
Or another and we too will perhaps
Weep, in spite of tears, get knocked about
Look foolish, spectacles fall off the nose
Grope blindly for a lost lens or the Holy Ghost,
Plead for sleep, rest, be denied it,
— Christ was given the bitter sop
To quench the thirst of his agony —
We're reading here of the little
Details that break a man
The little details like the tiny
Drop of water that drips hour by hour
Minute by minute into the bucket of
Timelessness and leaves a tremendous
Reverberation that echoes through the skull
Night after night and a night without sleep
Is all that's left of a lifetime.

The logos of creation

Who pronounced the logos of creation
That turned the world into a charnel house
The brightness of the shooting star falling
To earth hardens into shaft of stony light
Searing the breast and throat of all
That comes within its path an universe destroyed
Is hurled a burning ember in a sea of blood
The boulders rear their blackened humps
The oceans churn strange cannibal fish
That gulp their spawn devour their kind
Bloated with blood crawling upon the fungus
Of the waves livid with sickening putrefaction
As if the grave had yielded all
Retching up corpses from its bed;
The dolphins surge upon the storm
A froth of blood spurts from the guts
Harpoons of wind pierce the wave
The sea heaves and turns its belly upwards
Struck with a mortal wound, the monstrous
Sharks follow their sharp instinct
Snouting the odours of the jetting blood
The mountains split asunder by their
Inward fires, the forest falls, the trees
Swirl with tentacles hideous in greed
To grasp and clutch the struggling bodies
Spewed out by the poisonous breath of caves
Foetid with the breath of the dying and the dead.

Death sculptures

The bone chiselled by bullets into a fine
Sculpture swings from the crowded gibbets
On the plains, the bodies strewn upon the
Beach chill in glacid moonlight before
The sunrise gives them false warmth
But not to live or breathe, death
Dissembles the onlooker strolling idly
On the strand to clear the brain
Of tortured screams uttered by
Sequestered nightbirds in their cells
Whose claws wrenched off now lie
Heaped upon the tousled sand
Columns of ants crowding
On their dishevelled wing
New oyster beds explored by
Bodies of the plummeting dead
Blow open to spill out from
Within the nacreous flesh
Seething pearls of black and red

Night camp

The cindered fireflies shaken from the trees
Fall, black rain among the parched cicadas,
The antennae of moths and insects burnt off
Fumble in the dark faltering among the wounded
Lying with their fingers pressed against their
Wounds staunching the flow of blood
As their lives drip slow as from an hourglass
Through the sand falling drop by drop to nourish
Thorns, the fire dying out rustles, the ashes
Drop settling on the crumbling wood,
They have not known sleep for long
Dreams crawl worming through the brain
Coil in the interstices of the mind
Breeding from the seed of thought
That quivers faintly into bloodied root
Their eyes never close, the heart explodes
All they know is that death comes tomorrow
Now the wind blows through the fretting trees.

Naked they bathe in the springs

Naked they bathe in the springs
Wipe the bone clean of blood
Let the sap seep slowly back within
The marrow feel the water gush
Through rock, cleanse the flesh
That has long been polluted by
The stench of death bare their
Wounds to the sun, red flowers
That stunned the dark now fade with light,
Blood leaps and dances,
The reddened water flows
Clear, their folded shadows
Unfurl themselves and lengthened
Stretch whole upon the strand,
The sea walks with them on the shore
The tall waves rear to touch
Their crowns, the armies of the dead
Remove their spectral garments
Riddled through with bullets to the bone
Take on the aspect of the living
As the thunder of the battle
Recedes behind the dunes
Necrophilic lovers from each other
Turn away, unclasp their hands
Free their bodies from the fettering arms
Their long sleep with death is over,
But now more terrible more awesome
The dark eyes turned towards the living
Remembering the burning flambeaux
Of a thousand eyes closed and blind in death,
Buried in the dark.

Narcissus

The image in the mirror is no longer important
An echo haunts a legend's recollection,
Who else was there for Narcissus to love
But self and self's reflection, all nature
Was his glassy pool, even the water breathed
And pulsed at wink of eyelid and of lash,
The ripple gazed, took shimmer from the dazzle
Of his eyes, eddies fed his mouth
With kisses of his own creation,
Obsessions die and time leaves no retrieval,
An image fades etiolated
By its own voluptuous dreamings
Curdles the pool, gathers the scum
On weeds slimy, tangling over
Light of dwindling moon or sun.
Dragonflies drown buried beneath thunder
And fish, shredded by feeding beaks
Leave a white fern of bones on rock, for wreath.

No longer the image in the mirror
Teases thought, enamoured by incestuous passions
Where self entwined with self becomes
Its own inamorata, now the mirror shows
A myriad faces and through their eyes
Appear a thousand others to tantalise
And set ablaze the frozen fire of silver vein.
Time reveals to a heart estranged
Friends that are ghosts and lovers strangers.
Suddenly the pool grows black
The eyes that watch, close
Blind in darkness and the mirror cracks.

Mother-in-law

I find there is nothing new to learn
From their arrogance and their stories of the past
Refusal to admit to the truth of anything
Accept change, feeding the crows with balls of rice
Taken from her plate before she eats the first mouth
Lurching unsteadily into the garden staggering on pebbles
The golden orioles fly away, the crows pursue

'It is for Swami,' she says
'That is what Yogaswami has told
'You people all are gulping down your food
First before thinking of the gods
It is our custom to give the first mouth to the gods
The crows are the vahanam of Sani,' she says.

The crows flap about with waiting wings
To swoop down with raucous beaks
Picking at god-food. It is the daily dana.
Who am I to forbid the gods to feed at my pots
And pans,
'Look, the crows are coming right into the kitchen' I say
'Yes, it is so every day now' the maidservant says
'Next time I will eat all. If you don't want
Then I won't give.'
The stray dog sniffs at the food sometimes
Comes in muttering 'No fish, no meat so even
Dog will not eat.'
She is pure vegetarian won't touch Christian
Meat, egg, fish
'You all are flesh eaters' she says with disdain
'Achchi, do not call us flesh eaters' says the grand-daughter
'Flesh eaters? I said flesh-eaters? Those are
People who are eating human flesh, no?
In Africa they are called cannibals.
I did not say. Oh alright then I am
Eating, eating all day fish and meat
And purging purging.' Raises her voice
Becomes deaf to rationale. Begging bowl!

'Beggars. I am old dog. No use to anybody
Can't scrape a coconut half even.
Yes, yes they said let them keep her now
Now it is his turn. They said first
You must ask permission from lady of the house
It is the son's duty to look after the mother
It is not the duty of the son-in-law.
If you all can't keep put me in the
Naki madama I will go there
Very good very good
They said wait and see in six weeks
They will chase her away,' chuckles with
Ironic glee, that the prophecy has not been
Fulfilled does not move her one bit.

Her fingers flick sweetness to the tongue
Her lips pucker with little gasps at chillie
Her hands move over her food with the delicacy
Of fingers tracing alponas and kolam
On the threshold of her life the barren
Patch before the breaking structure of her house
Patterns that weave through the famine of her age
Into gnarled branches and withered leaves
The grains going awry, the magic of ritual
Dispersed so that no new rains come
No new harvests begin
And the scarecrows in the starving fields
Cry with toothless mouths to the parching wind

The purificatory rites she is reluctant to perform
Curving palm over forehead and throat to feel
Fire where there is only ice
'Fever I have today' she says 'I won't take bath today'
You all are very clean. Like Brahmins.
Your servant maid also is clean like lady of the house,
Very sensitive no! Sometimes cleaner than house people
I am like a piece of stinking dried fish, kunu malu'
Stings her haggard flesh with her own vituperation

Still the rubies like pomegranate seeds split
Her ear lobes the skin now like brown kahata
And the brilliant in her right nostril glitters
A vanishing beam of a lost firefly.

'Use coconut husk to scrub me' she says
'But you will not make my skin white.'
She makes profound statements
About the English language to Miyuki
'English is the greatest language in the world
Everybody in the world know English
Even in Africa they all speak English, no?
Which country you are from?' she continues
'Japan? Ah, in Japan there is great pagoda
Did you know Toya Menka Kaisha?'
'Where you are studying? You want to know
Who am I? I am their father's
Mother' she says pointing to the grandchildren
'My son, luv marriage
They met in University
My son in England also
Luv marriage,' pointing to a photograph
Of her grandchildren she says with pride
'Just like English children, no?'

'Old people' she says, 'We are old people
We are from Jaffna. We are from the village.
We have to come here to learn manners.
Etiquette. We criticize everything
We never say thank you. We are only saying
Too much uppu in that and this
We do not praise'
Her eyes sparkle with irony
Flicks us off like dust off her toes

Every evening she reads her prayer books
Gazing at each page as if it is the face of God
Sometimes prays to her grandchildren

96

When they bring her cups of coffee
With folded palms 'Siva' she says
'Darling. Rasathi.' She soon forgets
Endearments, the honey tilts off her tongue
The mouth becomes a starved bee.

Picking up her son's horoscope
Turns the leaves. 'Good time for my son,' she says
'Very brilliant period. Very high position.
Everybody obey him.'
Says the grand daughter, 'Where is all this?'
'That is what I say!'
Then she prays and says
'Anyway no problem with house?
Fever gone down? Amma sleeping?
Poor thing she is resting. Very tired no?
Parvum. Working hard no.'

Her legs curve bowed into limping
By the weight of carrying six children
Or at birth left unstraightened
Feeding at the bosom of her wet nurse
'Achchi you have Sinhala blood,
You drank milk of a Sinhala woman.'
'Who told you that? A Sinhala nona
Gave me milk. They all were
Respectable Sinhala nonas.'

Six children she did not give to wet nurses
Fed the weak one with tender chicken breast
Cracked tiny bones so that he suck marrow
To fill the hollows in his chest.
The others, she quailed from, eldest son
Leader, authority wielder, the whip curling over
The heads of the family, grasping every possession
First ball, first bicycle, first car, first trip abroad
First to touch food at table,
Daughters offered in marriage as wealth from

Family coffers, decked in attiyal and mukuthi
The other sons broke away
'They took wives and went' she says
'It is the duty of sons to look after the mother.'
She re-iterates.

That her first grandson died
At twenty three she does not know
Watching him talk to the cousins
One day she is proud
'Aney, just like a lawyer
He can argue no,' she says.

Does not ask for love
When her son is angered she says
'Temper just like my husband no!
Sometimes follows the grand daughter
To her room lifts clothes to fold
And put away, stands, watches never
To say that she is lonely, all she says is
'I want company. I am crow.'
And once in praise of the daughter-in-law
'Ah, she is poet, like Avuyair
It is talent from god no?
It is very blessed thing.'

Drought in Maho

The village is an anthill
Assailed by wounding tusk   marauding
Wildboar   elephant maddened with
          Must
The months are silver with drought
Loola fish burrow deeper
Into crevices of heat flagellated earth
Where the fat tubers of olu and nelun
          Perish
While light grows transparent
          On tapering buffalo
          Horn   spirals of sambhur
          Antlers curl in blue smoke
          Through the smouldering Vanni forest

The lemon tree stings
Viper sharp the pungent senses
          Where night reels through the
          Crickets endless padha
An empty winnowing fan
          Placed against earth —
— Wall of the hut
Black globules of gecko
          Eyes spill within the
          Woven interclasp
          Of dried reed
          The waterpot filled
          With grasshoppers sliding
          Through light   in rooms green
          With the seasons glow worms

The black mapila
          Curls round the ochre
          Red paddy bissa   scorpions search
          The dry fields by the anthill
          Village   fleshprint of foot
          tatooed with blue venom

99

In our garden
   There is water only in our well
   Many footpaths lead from the village
Across the fields   crossing the tracks
   Of the wild hare and the
   Thalagoya
At night each segment
Of field
         Brings the nariyas cry
         Closer to our shelter
         In the thatched roof of the village huts
         Beyond the fields
Reptiled scales rustle
Through reed flutes
Of straw

My father the old hunter
Brings out the mazed nests
   Of weaver birds
   And shrine offerings of grain
   But there is no whisper
   Of rain where the wavulas
   Ravage the green mangoes

The golden antlers
Of ancient rituals
   Settle on my father's head
   Together we explore the forest
Beyond we explore
   The wewa
Watching thought the sambhur's delicate
   Rib cage
   A waterhole shrunk into the
   Dimension of a
   Dark pupilled eye
   Suck in shadows
   Of elephant and leopard

Above the empty wewa
The eagle rises from the
Bo-tree roots in the firedry
Forest its talons
Strongly clasp the slumbering python
    Feeding in the forest
    Sated with herb sweet deer
    Flesh

Mother

She baked cottage loaves on the old cast iron stove
Fed with coke and coal from the railway yard
Beautifully rounded they were crusty top-knotted
Glazed smooth as brown eggshells crackling to the touch
Cut in thick slices and spread with Mrs Tilly-
From-upcountry's-butter golden yellow pats
Sliding palm cool out of their green clover leaf
Emblemed packs Mrs Tilly from some English
County village in the dales up now in the mists
Swirling on the patana grass mountains
Those rich pasture lands where her
Milch cows grazed, Ayrshires and what-not,
Packing her cloves scented memories into her
Butter churns

Brought home when my father took the trains
On the upcountry line, kept in watercooled
Butter dishes while the tins of jam, plum,
Apricot, blackcurrant, lemon and melon
Pungent with ginger brought all the way on
Those Cunard Liners, labelled with the exotica
Of English orchards, placed on brimming saucers
Clustered with sweet-seeking pomander balls
Of red ants,

Outside, on the hill top, and in the garden,
The ripe mangoes pressed their juice against
The bursting skins and the jak fruit cleft with
Ripeness split, crashing, its flesh
Sweet as honey crawling with red dimiyas
All sorts of flowers yielded pollen for the bees
In their blue painted hives, honeysuckle pale yellow
And those lush cream roses with never a blush
On their petals virginal fresh with dew traced
Pink veins breathing in their own fragrance
A curious finger ever so slightly slides aside
The shutter to view a gempit spill of crawling
Tourmalines topazes and alexandrites all

Shimmering in the sun; smoked out they swarm-
Cloud and lay a lash of stings upon your flesh,
Needleshaft thorns prised out and rubbed
With lime and white chunam you feel your
Body broken into like some halved wax comb
Dripping all over with bee jelly and honey.

In the evening the bamboo tats pulled down
Sitting by the glow of the glass globed lamp
She would read to me stories of enchantment,
Of castles, Windsor and Balmoral, of English
Nannies and of a princess named Lillibet
Outside in the thumbergia bowered garden
The night insects shrilled and the praying mantis
Lifted its stick legs in a stately gavotte on the
Windowsill, the gecko wayangs began their
Nightly shadow play and my mother searched for the
Hidden cricket chirping away, hidden in the folds
Of our white nightgowns its time tick emerging
Out of the white washed wall until she captured
It in the folds of the pillowcase and shut her ears
To its persistent chiruppings,

She did not talk of her dreams as I did, lent her
Ears to our prayers as we knelt at her knees she
Sitting on the valanced four-poster and her daughters
On either side of her knees already the Bali drums
Starting up in the village of exorcists and the flames
Leaning through the air flung like orange
Red marigold garlands on the shoulders of the dark hill
Of Belungala.

In Lillibet's garden there were no terrors
And night owls hooting the daffodils and crocusses
Bordered the trimmed lawns,

In mine there were a myriad creatures
Earwigs crawling at my ear and millipedes scuttling
And slithering like metallic railtracks, creatures
With stings and feelers, antennae and shells and

103

Caterpillars lining the tiles with their black moss
The green reptiles twining in the passion fruit creepers
When it dawned, the cock bird crowing in Mr Cowie's
Garden I woke to a day without hours, a clock
Without hands and felt the years pass only when
My chintz dress grew tight at the armpits, with
Hems that must be let down, the buttons hanging
On a single thread before they fell off and rolled
Under the leopard skin in the hall.

My knees green with crushed herbs pressed
Against raw wounds and grazes as I fell on that
Stony pathway along the tea bushes walking among the
Leeches in the long grass that clung to my flesh
Red lanterns glowing incandescent with my blood

A thimble on her finger she stitched folds of Irish
Linen for her sheets tucked under the cotton mattresses
And I, standing by her, turning the wheel of her old
Sewing machine; she was to me often a mystery
As I was to her, I knew that I sought her warmth
Often by flinging myself on her lap, I soon grew
Too heavy for her and she grew weary of telling me
Stories so I dreamed my own fictions.

When I was ill she propped me among pillows
Placed an ice-bag on my forehead and fed me with gruels,
Syrups of crystal sugar from the kitul flower
And juice of the sour orange, placed in my hands
The little knotted bundle of kalu duru seeds
To sniff at, breathed in from basins hot with
Steam and clouds of orange Friars Balsam while I chewed
Valmi twigs so bitter sweet, rubbed liniments upon my
Chest and wrapped me in the warmest wools while the
Sun blazed outside and the garden lay like a tortoise
Feeling its earth shell grow warm, the ladybirds
Red and black and gold spilling from little jewel boxes
Filigreed with sun.

On the stone verandah with the green tats rolled up
The barber shingled my hair, he had a squint and smelt

Of talcum powder strong and cheap, the sheet tucked
Round my neck he left me shorn like some helpless
Sheep tossing off clumps of black wool digging the
Cold scissors onto my ears and drawing blood from
The tiny earlobes as I sat imprisoned on the old
Victorian feeding chair.

I watch Mrs Macdonald scrub Heather's calves
And knees with a soapy flannel
'That's not the way my mother washes me' gravely
I pronounce,
'And how does she wash you then?' asks Mrs Macdonald,
The wife of Engine Driver Macdonald
Came all the way from some far Scottish Highland
Village, living here in this little township beneath
The shadow of Dawson's tower, listening to the
Shunting of trains and the long whistle of engines
At the railway crossing,
'She fills a tub with water and baths me'
I say, 'the water is warm, I am soaped all
Over, she pours water over my body enfolds
Me in a big towel.' Holds fragrant incense in
My room to ward off chills;
And often I sink into the cotton bin
Pressing myself further and further in
Until I feel myself the fleece clutched
Within the seared brown pod, the seed
Tickling me and cobwebby strands netting
My sun warmed body, soon this cotton
Will fill the pillow that I sleep on
As I lie, night after night on the jakwood
Four-poster,
And stories of her own life, there were many
That she told me, stories dark with the
Thunder of death and fear but it was
Always me whom she led out of danger
When the high wind rose and the boat
Capsized in the lagoon lifted me high
Above the water and then again
When one dark night she fled with me

Across the fields clutching me, an infant in her
Arms;

And Mrs Cramer comes to see me, old lady in black
Crepe, black cotton stockings and black buckled leather
Shoes, her black hat skewered with a steel pin
Her face all seamed with age her hands her palms
With earthcracks, draught fissures of soil toiling
On her land searching for brides for her sons.
'I must find a Convent girl, orphan with crucifix
Dangling between her breasts and a rosary tucked in at
Her waist, some foundling left basketed on the steps,
A girl who would dig and hoe and boil the pot of
Rice with kindling wood, escape from being a parlour girl,

'You will be a queen one day
You will be a queen one day' she intoned
But those oracles seemed to a child
So far away.

Search my mind

'You can't ask questions of a man with a gun'
(Character from the play 'Camps')

But you cannot search my mind
That bears the peeling architecture of a city
Being gradually razed to the ground
Its bubble towers, pavilions and palaces
Disintegrating in the spiralling whorls of smoke
You cannot see its waterways once used
For casual river traffic boats and rafts
Poling against currents setting out on leisurely journeys
Of carrying goods, netting some fish on the way,
Now bearing its floating merchandise
Thrown overboard to rot, grow putrid
Feeding the gluttonous fish that tear
Both hair and entrails,

You, young soldier order me to get off
Scuttle out of my seat, show my bag, its shabby
Contents exposed — books, small change, poems that no one
Reads — walk past you, suffer the inconvenience
Of any traveller in this time of war,
'Get down,' you order, young soldier
Standing for hours, bored, among the spilling
Sandbags, the tousled pillows of a battlefield
I watch you filling your kettle at the water tap
And glimpse your austere iron bedsteads
Ranged within the khaki tent, marooned
Upon your island between a silent campus
Strewn with hacked off heads and a
Flowering garden brilliant with fountaining
Jets from which you're cordoned off
Your innocence squandered as easily as
Bullets, your energies spent to leave
Your life like empty cartridge cases
Strewn upon this desert earth, our past times
Were less dangerous than your death
Picnics, camping upon the ledge of

107

Mountains where eagles flighted
You have no time for all this, young soldier
Sound your bugle loud and clear
Your weapons, aim at air, trained at
The soaring falcons, you fret at birds
That strip the grain off harvest fields
Shoot the twittering sparrow and intrusive blackbird
While Death, the scarecrow stares and grimaces,
A dancing spectre whose stuffed straw body
Ignites, flares into flame, its ash scoffing at the
Sun, blinding the eye in a field that's burned,
Despoiled.

We have our genealogies

We have our genealogies but what do they mean?
Nothing. They tell us, those historians that our beginnings
Were invasions, that we walked through blood trails
Sucking like leeches the rich ruby that spilled
From gempits of flesh; we wore those blood splotches
Like jewels sparkling on our wrists, our breasts.

Flesh still cries for the power of that beauty
Reflected in the flashed blood mirrors,
That show our image bathed in its glitter while, tied
To the stake, conflagrations of heretics blaze away
As the fire faggots ignite crackle before they topple,
Fall like great silver candle sconces

Sometimes wearing nailcrowns hammered into the
Skull before they roll away scattered helter skelter
As in a game of bowls on a well trimmed lawn,
Invasions were nothing compared now to the taste
Death has for these hedonists, lovers of torture
And all its titillations of necrophilic flesh, suddenly
To turn voluptuary as the groin screams and the
Air breaks apart into tremendous glass fissures
As the power enters them to speak in tongues
As on the Day of Pentecost, in a language only the
torturer understands,

Saliva blots the lips that are now still, silenced,
A forgotten script bitten into chiselled stone
And no one cares to pause so much as to kick
Even with a blunt naked toe that has walked
Always barefoot over so much rutty terrain —
The path knotted with chains of corpses.

You find yourself wandering demented through
Feudal gardens were the frozen serfs rolled off
Pedestals flesh turning to marbled ice as the
Snow fall mantled the black firs
It was only the great manor houses that shook

With the lights of a thousand candles as the sky
A heavy branched candelabra swung with stars,
Read me again those pages that tell of Azavedo
Of Westerwold, of D'Oyly, those diaries in archives of
Centuries which dwell like so many silver fish malingering
Among the parchment scrolls like mummified skin,

What's flung in your face are the documents
Written on leaves of flesh as on the ola leaves
Of ancient temples, yellow-brown, brittle, stiff
And the lettering so richly archaic so scholarly
Scripted with the fine tools torture has etched.

Murals

There is so much poetry around us now with the talking
Walls reaching out to us, the great new Jackson
Pollocks muralling our city, we walk through barriers
Seeing our new identities at checkpoints, assuming new
Shapes and forms, faces that turn pallid as dead
Wax flowers within cloudy glass domes;

Rapid scripts form in our minds a stammer of
Dialogue or silence that makes us snail retract
Into the shell we knew to be so brittle;

From ancient costume boxes we pull out a motley
Of garments reclothing our chameleon flesh disguised
To take new roles playing down the histrionics of our
Loose gestures and curbing the fluent tongue
Teaching it the new deceptions speaking within
Our throats those endless silent soliloquies
Somewhat carelessly looking into the barrels of
Guns and noticing off handedly that the lips
Of the young soldier are chiselled finely like the
Statue of David or Apollo in some Roman square;

They have to mean something to us, those great
Stark canvasses as we read them on our
Saga journeys, behind them a wall of bodies
With eyes screaming at us and silent mouths
Offering us the signs of the times, death couriers,
Messengers of Armageddon their prophecies usher
In the new annals of history.

Their spontaneous scholarship has penned
Epistles to the new converts, their brushes
Swept across decaying structures, bold
Calligraphies jutting out to strike the eyeballs
With swords of paint,

One day perhaps the plains wide and empty will be
Swept clear of carrion flesh, the long brooms

Lift off the streets sopping wet with blood, bone
Splinters sift under the earth stratified eras of
History fossilized in onyx or jade
Now as you walk through a deserted courtyard
The pomegranates split, skull blood dripping
And you remember this fleeting instant prisoners
Who killed pigeons for food;

Listening to the explosions reverberate through the clouds
You wonder whether the hunters have shot down
A covey of birds while our long drowsing
Afternoon nap is disturbed as much as Skanda's
Was in that wild stampede in the temple to
Find to his surprise his vestments stained and botched
With penetential blood that flowered from breast and groin.

Tied to the stake these new martyrs ignite
Like faggots and blaze away burnt for their
Heresies, in this new witchcraft, worshippers
Of the powers of darkness; decapitated too.
Time turns over pages of history to show us
Heads lolling off gibbets, bodies wrenched
Apart by falling trees, elephant trunks
Hurling you into the sands and flesh shreds
Like votive flags fluttering among twirled
Bones twisting in the sand.

Bone landscape

The sun calcifies those structures ossiferous walls
Through which the fire enters is then this body
The hearth on which the pot settles to boil
And froth with milk?

Auspicious festivals of death begin, continue,
Remember the kneeling with palms clasped
Together like lidded urns which presage their
Ashes
Remember too the magical enchanted herbs
Pressed on your head, the oil pouring like
An oblation of gold sovereigns to blessing,

You believed with all the others in promised
Harvests the New Year would bring, the rice
Plump with milk bursting on your tongue
And your shadow once so puny billowing out
To mock the starveling scarecrow;

The beak of the cuckoo clashes against the door
Of your life and the death knell is heard
In its cry, this spring then will read
To you new symbols, the season interpret
the bird omens and gecko chirpings
And death shadows slide through your limbs
The cobra chill touching your loins and you,
Eyes blindfolded, hands knotted behind your
Back already feel the crater flow of lava
Spill out from your sundered skull
The sky splits with scarlet lesions and the
Bruised clouds puff out thunderdark.

We knew you once bathing at the well
In the paddyfield the scarecrow grimacing
With the spectral head swallowing spit and
Casting its evil eye, gaping at the body
Laved in sunlight, the crystal chains of
Water beads pouring in a glitter over a supple

Neck and you were there by the river swimming
With the fish while the kabaragoya lurked
Among the marsh reeds waiting for its promised
Repast; we knew you, but you knew nothing
Of us, our lives you said, were separate,
We were the hedonists lifting fruit to our
Lips and spiced meats off garnished platters
Gulping all kinds of liquors, mulled wines
And mead, liqueurs from vineyards and orchards
As we lolled on voluptuous couches emptying
Perfume flacons to conceal the stench of death
That rises miasmic from the burning streets,
Stretching our toes that never felt dust or spittle
Or blood from the abattoirs,

There are memories of course, dawn in the city
And the thin ribbed cattle being led to slaughter,
Their hooves clopping on the tarred road by
the shawl covered men rapping their sticks on the
Cringing fly wracked hides,
They could not veer off being roped, tethered
For execution and the grass cud they chewed
Was already blackening into turds; soon their
Carcasses clotted with blood would swing off
The hooks in the market place and their entrails
Spill out like silver snail trails, blood
Creased out of flesh folds flooding the buckets,
A bloodied palm clutch — offering to the populace
A heart, a brain, liver, lights, while the meat
Fed dogs shaggy with fur, scramble for offal
And the cooking pots in humble homes sizzle with fat.

The landscape now has new signposts which no
One regards, whose face it is or body becomes slowly
Unrecognizable and the fires never go out as
If the ghosts of Vestal Virgins have returned
To set up in our streets, new temples.

Only the mangy dogs are finally happy
As they chew into the choicest delicacies

114

Gnawing the bone clear of once sweet flesh,
Lost its fragrance and aroma, seared and burnt
Like fruit bats they cling to branches
Crepitatious maggots seething in each orifice
Chrysalises spinning hairstrand threads for
The monstrous larvae to hatch out
The Deaths Head moths.

Passages

I should be dead by now or thought of as some
New migrant poet shaking the dust off my feet
And kissing foreign soil but, I am neither,
Trying out, instead of chartering
Some new route to safety or escape, new dance
Steps for a phantom costume ball wearing those
Clothes, heavy with their mothball scent that once
Belonged to youthful summers, unrehearsed those shrouds
That wrap our spectres, put new meat upon these
Bones so starkly marionette in stance and gesture,
Stepping out in fancy dress we wore to tread
In stately minuettes, move as ghost through mirrored
Walls that float their bubble images to burst and
Disappear, fleshless as time, waltzing through
A spectral world in crinolined skirts fichued in
Tulle, a sprig of orchids at our breast;

That was no time to mourn, then how do we remember
Joy, only a single thread snarled between the
Insterstices of those ruined pillars
Leaves its brilliant silk caught between
The edge of teeth that bite on memory
Trapped like kingfisher
In snaring net;

That I am still alive makes my return, time's
Ghost, to lift the stones off from the breast of
Martyrdom to speak for all whose breath is
Less than vapour in a misty dawn, whose
Bodies no enchanted herb can bring to life
Yet whose flesh and blood transubstantiates
Our thought to make us new converts,
Communicants who once more lift the chalice,
Break the bread and celebrate the suffering
Of the Cross;

Watch violence through the telescope of years, feel
My life flat, a trampled shadow as the hobnailed

116

Boots tramp over and over again covering new terrain
Freshly conquered; know fear chill as a clammy toad
Perched on my belly feel the gnaw of night rats
In my sleep, the quiet louse that feeds within the armpit,
Have thought of exile, dig many times over
My own grave hearing the thump fall of heavy sod
Tumbling in its quick descent within the pit;

Yet all these years those strangers at my gate
With whom I had no kinship either of flesh or tongue
Stood outside those half closed windows watching us
At our strange charades as we gravely danced to
Music each step taking us further and further
Back into deepening shadow away from curious eye.

We were birds of a feather, yes, flocking in that
Closed sanctuary, thought that no one would displace
Us, our lives pulled out in secret like those
Hidden gifts from Christmas stockings full of strange
Surprises, snowballs and nuts, apples and books
With gilded pages, searched deep to find whether
Our lives could see reflections in other lives
And faces, however humdrum, walk into
Country cottages or manor house or cowslip meadows;

Outside those walls the deep drains filled with
Blood from abattoirs, the huge clay pots simmered
With meats slipped off the hooks, black rugs of
Tripe, rallipallams of entrails and intestine,
Bloodied heads and hearts and slaughtered flanks
Of beasts while we sat down and feasted
— With starched white damask napkins
Spread upon our knees and silver forks and knives
That cut those silvery slivers into delicate morsels
To whet our finicky appetites — grasped in our fingers.

One hears now, yet one has always heard, death
Rattles in the throat of those who die, those of our
Kin and gently as they breathe their last we feel
That peace, their peace since they no longer suffer;

117

It is the end for them, for us the wait begins
This time for our own selves, ancestral dreams
Now haunt us and we study curious as a bunch
Of sight seers come back to visit colonies of lost
Empires the flagstones of old churches slabbed
With ancient tombstones, plaques, memorial tablets
Names, dates, epochs of conquest that have gone
To sleep sunk in the comfort of four-posters,
Rust-banks, stretched out beside a wall
Where lizards creep on ratanned chaise-longues;

Here then, we stop short, take breath and
Wonder what records our bitter, nameless
Silence leaves behind as we join that vast
Concourse of sated worms fed with rich
Sermons from a predikanten's mouth.

Metaphors of history

Louvais nos per Deos
Este grande Dia
Ja nasce senhor
Per virgin Maria

It is perhaps now only a taste on the tongue
Remembered, lingering where it once blent so
Easily with that other language to bubble milk-
Frothing at our lips drunk from those scalding
Pans set on the hearth, tasting of woodsmoke
Flames flushed out from husk and crackling
Frond and shell

A taste of spice, sugared fruit, a sweetness
Laid upon the tongue and palate, festivities
Of richness in that grand Crismis spread

    Amor, te droemi sonoe regelado
    Anjoes rodiando folga juntado

Pastried crispness melting in the mouth
Brought smoking hot from sizzling pans
Straight off the fire poured thick with syrup,
The table set with dishes, platters piled high
With pente frito, fougetes filled with succulence
Of amber fruit-flesh crusted with crystallised
Frost of sugar, boroa and bol-fiado,

Country flavours too, roasting fowls turning
On spits stuffed with piquant herbs, the hot
Spiced pastole meats lashing the taste buds
As the tongue smarts stung with pepper, tart
With tamarind, steaming rice piled hot-hot on
China dishes and hoppers baking in pans
Fresh eggs golden yolked settling like small
Suns in milky white clouds

A language you could eat and drink
In that rich ritual of feeding

A fragrance smelt, lifted to nostril of hot
Dark cloves and cinnamon scrolls crushed
With powdered nutmeg and milky cadjus,
Nuts pounded within the alabaster bowl
Impregnate with essence of rose and almond,

Aromatic as herbs which sprang so readily
From the soil of its adoption, seed scattered
By some migrant wind or bird to grow into
A bush or vine laden with coffee bloom or
Berry.

Shaking a memory-till within my hands,
Palms clasped round its cool, clay sides
Incised with fern and vine, silver or copper
Coins strike echoes against its walls, a motley
Jingle, fanams and zeraphims, larins and cents
And shillings, here and there a stuiver or two
Hoarded through the years to yield the purchase
Of a birthright, money carefully unwound from
Knotted store tucked into waist or bodice
With its edge of tatted lace to be exchanged
For provender sundry things like meat or fish
Or eggs, fine powdered sugar, muslin, thimbles, thread

I hear still that xylophonic music at Christmas
Time, spoons acrobatically placed one upon the other
And touched to set bells jingling in silver
Carillons or strummed on bandarinhas, strange,
Strange to my ears now their voices lilting as
They spoke or sang, taking the language of
Their new conquerors, they were the metaphors of
History, strands of bright thread from
Jacob's coat of many colours, opening my window
To their carols

   Amor si ten Sanoe, Amor,
   Nos nao fai aballoe;
   Mais, si ten cordado, Amor.

Why should we lose that patois, let it be
Forgotten, neglect that bird, the brilliant parrot
Pettapo, let it fall limp in history's tarnished
Birdcage with one last shake of emerald feathers
Dropped from its rich plumage, forget the memory
Of the bird that spoke the mimicries of myriad
Tongues,

Why museum that poetry, make its form archaic
Laid aside to gather dust worn out with us
A viaule with its strings snapped off
Flung in some attic lost in dissonant echoes,

Whole oyster beds opened to reveal those pearls
From which those priceless revenues were
Culled, those divers speeding through the siphoned
Waves tunnelling to ocean bed weighted each
With his taxed stone, the sea knives shimmering
With scales prised open shells and lustre
Seeds spilled out later to adorn the ears of some
Fidalgo's lady love,

Who remembers now the harlequinry of their dress
The chaste buttoned bodices tucked and trimmed
With lace, their long looped braided hair set
With jewelled kooras as they danced in quaint
Ritual of love and courtship through the past's
Long, dark passageways, singing their chicotis,
Bowing and courtseying in those stately cafferinhas?

Cingalee Nona! Cingalee Nona!
En kera kasa
Porta ninhere, orta ninhere
Figa namas da
Figa names da none
Figa namas da.

Orchards and gardens burgeoned with
Laden vines of fruited loves, their progeny

121

Bursting forth like melon seeds to gourd
The thirsty land with sweetest flesh

Peering through windows in those narrow
Streets the listening ear strains to
Catch those melodies that time so
Gently draws away from those salons
To graveyard wedded with spectres and with ghosts

> 'Peeping through the window darling
> What will people say,
> If you want to marry me darling
> Come the proper way.'

Theirs too was a nation, that with conquest
Over many now with ease, would have, forgotten,
Yet each new conquest-blood, finds names
Prolonging that inheritance, hybrids that spread
Their roots, their vines clustering with glossy
Grape, like rubies red and white cusped
And carapaced in time,

Even after maps had perished, the rotting
Ships scuttled or wrecked, the old sea routes
Where once the waves shimmered like rich
Silk, crushed and tattered by merchant-men
Jostling for room, the one-time conquerors
Anonymous in history's market place, their
Pockets empty of xeraphims and pardaos
No longer to purchase their slaves and souls,
Yet their off-shoots still remain, enrich the
Soil bear many names engraved — if time
Builds tombs upon the mind — remind us of
The Mikko kind, the Laffai Burgher,
Ambachstlieden,

Yet gentle mockery makes them kin to us
Who like them shake exotic plumage
Chirping in tongues, flaunting with pride
Our feathers to colonise, replenish with our

Mating cries the procreate aviaries, once
In that past, so well stocked by some conquistador
Who laid aside his armour for a while to
Rest upon the wayside, drink his coconut wine
Take time off from writing those records in
Thombos, allowed the ink to dry before
Once more he laboured over dues and
Lands and services or like those maraleiros
Collecting their death taxes journeyed through
Villages eating and drinking with the people
Filling their pouches with larins and guilders

We then are left pausing from our travels
To decipher that Rosetta stone lost in time-
Deserts, to find that language key entering the streets
they walked, the chambers they inhabited

Bon entrego de Nataal
Coen Caronne regelando

A Life
Displaced

A Life Displaced

*'La nature est un temple où de vivants piliers laissent parfois
sortir de confuses paroles; l'homme y va à travers des forêts de
symboles. On l'observe avec de familiers regards.'*[1]

Correspondance de Charles Baudelaire

*'As weeks follow one another, certain things happen without
actually being totally new to me. When they happen I have
already known about them. I have been expecting them. And with
my expectations being confirmed doubts of all kinds and colours
crop up in my mind. The result is a feeling that my life (the lives
of a million other people, perhaps all people) is predictable.
Everything is predictable: my past, my present and my future.
Mixed feelings of unrest, anguish, betrayal, pain and insecurity
assail me. Having someone peering at you from nowhere, reading
your life for you in snapshots is a terrible horror.'*

(From the Diary of Mohand)

I open the diary which he gave me as a gift of our friendship before he left for his country. The diary began with
both those lines from Baudelaire and their translation
extending themselves into his life and thoughts, his past
and his present, in a world which had yet to make its
destination known. In the pages which were to follow lay
that part of his life which revealed itself in dreams, conversations and the probings into that deep, painful *angst* which
was never to leave him.

Each page opened windows to the different view-scapes
in his life — the ridges and peaks of the Atlas Mountains
with its wind-blown trees where he went as a child to pick
firewood, the orchards of apples, apricots and peaches in
his home, the ksar in the desert with its mazes of rooms, the
bars in the city where he went to drink and the room in
which he had once lived, looking out onto the sea. This

---

[1] 'Nature is a temple where living pillars sometimes allow mysterious
words to arise; man goes through forests of symbols which observe him
with familiar eyes.'

room, with its wide windows, looked out upon a painting
by Klee with its hot Mediterranean colours and dark fronded
palms waving against the golden light that dissolved into
the azure of sea and sky. I heard the sound of the waves, of
the surf beating against the rocks and flowing onto the
beaches, but I could not see any ship that travelled over the
horizon. There was only a wide sky and the sea which could
presage shipwreck and the sirens, the lorelei waiting to
beguile him on the rocks.

The diary is an extension of his life. The story he begins
to tell me of his life. We were both strangers in that country
when we first met. It was late spring going into the bronze
and gold of autumn. He left before the summer had begun
and the daffodils were out so we shared a winter darkness
and the whiteness of snow-covered landscapes, valleys and
mountain peaks and the ice-bound streets which we trav-
ersed of our ordinary lives and our everyday journeys.

When autumn arrived the leaves in George's Square were
changing colour — russet, golden brown, yellow edged out
the green. The winds were beginning to sweep the leaves
off the branches which took off like a flock of birds sweeping into the air. The naked branches bared their arms to the
furious gales. When winter arrived they were limned with
white snow like soft white fleece lying athwart them — ice
ladies in fur coats. Autumn — the evenings grew darker,
the sky loured with thunder-grey clouds and the snow
flakes began to fall, slight flakes, so chill to the touch,
dissolving a tear of ice. The grey buildings, the church
spire, the streets, were enfolded in a sweep of feathery,
downy flakes until the roads and parks and gardens were
white with snow. A white mantle covered the hills which
were carpeted with purple heather during the summer. The
rivers and streams froze. Birds skated on floating islands of
ice in the stream that flowed through the park.

Then spring began to arrive, tentatively. The thaw set in,
the ice to crack and the bulbs that lay buried beneath the
earth began to push forth their green stalks out of the white
snow. Little clumps of flowers began to appear beneath the

trees; water slipped, gurgling over the stones and rocks in the reed-covered stream that ran through the University grounds and the daffodils appeared, golden with their petals spilling like egg yolk, brilliant in the pale sun. But that was a summer in which my friend was absent. He had gone back to his country. I walked through the green grass, I wanted to lie down and sleep or read on the fresh succulent grass but then I saw the dog turds and I had to walk past, searching for another spot. The students were sunning themselves on benches. The tulips were a blaze of colour in George's Square, bright ruby red and vermilion, orange, gold. And in the Royal Gardens the sun fell on bodies that seemed to have been wrapped up and swathed in skins and furs and pelts in their winter hibernation.

In George's Square the children ran about feeding the pigeons and people sat in deep contentment eating crisps out of paper bags. The bands played, the trumpet and cornet players, sang out, the wood-winds filled the air, the drum beat out its deep bass notes. The musicians wear bright clothes, coats red as the tulips; the sun shines on the brilliant silver instruments. The birds are returning, flocking together on the trees with their new leaves and shoots of tender green. It is the seasonal renewal and the sluggish blood begins to stir and awaken in the veins.

George's Square — the lonely ones sit here too. The soldier who has fought in several wars, sits companionless on a bench on Poppy Day with the coloured ribbons and medals emblazoning his chest. The wreaths of red poppies lie at the foot of the war memorial like clotted blood.

I walk briskly along those streets, alone but so much at home, sometimes speaking into a mike held out to me by someone who is interviewing people on a street for Scottish Television. I hear myself talking about myself, my experiences, to strangers and soon thousands of other strangers will hear my voice but never know me, never see my face.

I had turned, I remember, a corner of that same street and met him returning from one of his lonely journeys. We were both spending a vacation with the other foreign students in

129

one of the Halls in the University village. We were still more
or less strangers to each other. We smiled in recognition,
yet, respecting each others' need to make our private journeys, we stopped briefly to speak. I crossed over to the
pavement where he stood before I turned the next corner.
We stood before each other.

'I have just been to Le Chat Noir. I felt thirsty for a beer',
he said.

'I'm just drifting' I told him and walked on through
streets, not sure of any destination. It was cold. I went into a
shop that was having a bargain sale to buy warm clothes.

In the evening we sat and watched programme after
programme on television. There were three floors and three
different lounges so we moved from floor to floor watching
the programmes of our choice. Outside the lounge a Chinese
student was trying to make a long distance call to Hong
Kong. There were many lonely people here. You could have
moved back to your room and completed your assignments
or gazed out of a window watching the gentle dropping of
the snow flakes and the crystal shapes of icicle flowers
forming on your windowpane but sometimes you had to
hear the sound of a human voice. Mohand began to tell me
stories from his life like some Arabian story teller in the
market place, delving deep down into the mind store of
myth and legend to unfold scene after tantalising scene of a
world I knew nothing of, of a life I knew nothing of. They
were the first tentative lines that he began to write for me,
the enchantment and mystery of an unknown life that
waited to unfold its story. Our conversations became the
writing of our fictions and of our poetry, they were passages
in diaries, they were the letters that we received from an
unknown world of dreams. We were both spinning out the
long skeins of tapestry thread, unravelling our travellers'
tales and weaving fantastic landscapes of the countries of
our interior lives in which we began to take our first steps
together so that we would not feel the icy bite of loneliness
eating into our lives. For him it was always the exploration
of his *angst*, of his looking into his constant search for what

had always eluded him. He sits in a bar at Oujda, alone. The women come and go. They sit and talk endlessly to the men. 'I would see them talking,' he says. 'I didn't know what they were talking about. They would say things, speaking with animation, their eyes bright, their lips sliding like silk over the supple movement of bodies as if they wanted to keep silence for ever at bay. They talked feverishly looking into eyes which turned them out again onto the streets or into another bar or into one of those rooms with their tousled sheets flung all about on dishevelled beds. I remember one of those women. We sat at different ends of the bar. I looked into her eyes. There was nothing beyond those eyes but death. They were blank. They reminded me of the eyes of a man I had seen in a picture. Just the eyes looking out of darkness. Blankness and death. I was drunk, she was drunk. There was nothing behind those eyes. Twice I nearly committed suicide. Once I had taken Kif and had almost walked off the window ledge and the other time was when I was deeply, deeply affected emotionally.'

For me, our friendship begins with the stirring of pity when he tells me of the injustices of his grandfather. When he was four years old he had quarrelled with the son of one of his uncles. The grandfather had called Mohand and began twisting his ear, still twisting it, he led him into a room where he was put in and locked up for hours and hours, forgotten until his uncle found him where he lay in the darkness, unconscious. His mother told him that he slept for eight months after that experience. To me it seemed a going back into the womb for a further period of gestation at the end of which he emerged to live again. In a way it resembled my own second birth. I was still in the womb not yet ready to be born when the doctor had tried to make my mother give birth to me. I stubbornly clutched on to the blood-nourished comfort of that interior chamber until I grew and was ready to emerge at the correct time. I too had gone back to sleep, like the seed that needed the earth to nurture it so that it would germinate and put forth its shoot, wavering and uncertain into a world of light. It was a second journey that we both had to make in order to be human and whole again but we had both known the deep unconscious death of our senses and of our physical natures before our tears watered the arid plains and valleys to make the fields yield their harvests.

He talks of his mother who is a Berber. 'She is very charming' he tells me, 'but now she is old and her hair is white and yellow. She wove carpets and she made big round flat loaves of bread, baked in the clay oven. She makes cous-cous. A big mound of it is cooked. The sauce is poured over it as if to irrigate the dry earth. As the soil is made fertile for the seed to grow. It is stirred with a special spoon. My mother was married before and I have a step brother; he is fair like the Berbers. There are ten of us in our family. My father had four wives. He is tall. Still handsome. He led a picaresque existence and went to Algeria to work. Then he came back to Taourirte where he started making babies. I sometimes think of him as a criminal.'

'Why?' I ask

'He left his first wife and daughter. My grandfather forced him to leave that wife of his. He was sad but he had to listen to his father. Later on the daughter died. My father is a strong man. He wears a cap on his head and he sits and puffs through his mouth when he is talking, like this ffff . . . He grew the best roses, he was a gardener in the hospital and those roses were sent to France. He always dressed us well, we, his sons. We always wore fashionable clothes, good shoes. I remember the revolution in my country. I was very small. My father would always come and take me home after school. On that day he did not come. I went in search of him and I lost my way in the city. Everything was confusing. There was shooting, crowds running in all directions, noise. I didn't know which way to turn. It was a rebellion against the reigning monarch and the government troops were firing all around me. I could have been killed but suddenly a man took me by the hand and led me to his home where he gave me food and drink. He questioned me once I got over my fear, found out where

I lived and took me back to my parents.

"Why didn't you wait until I came for you", my father asked.

'If he got late to take me home I would be in tears. Ah, my memories as a child. So many of them. Once I had eaten too much of a whole roasted sheep. I ate until my stomach was overfull. I felt my stomach dissolving. The schoolmaster sensing my unease called my elder brother to take me home. He was angry, offended. He took me part of the way and kicked me. "Go home by yourself", he shouted and left me.

'I went home by myself. My mother took off my clothes and washed me tenderly. Yes, she's one of the kindest women I have known. She calls me Mohand. When I come to Midelt where my home is, she covers my face with kisses, she is so happy to see me. But she quarrels with her daughters-in-law. I will not interfere even when she appeals to me. She does not get on with my wife. One day I returned home to find my mother weeping. My wife had been harsh to her, she said. They quarrel when they are together. I won't forget the day my son Youssef was born. I had gone to a party and returned home late to find that she had got her pains. My wife's family would have killed me if anything had happened to her. It was just in time. We got a car and took her to hsopital. She had the baby. I went back and slept. My mother-in-law had got up and gone early to the hospital when I was asleep. I hated my mother-in-law, more than anyone, I hated her at that moment. She made me feel guilty. When I awoke I took chicken and fruit for my wife but my mother-in-law was angry with me because I had not gone early to see my wife.'

Yes, he had a wife, children, but they lived far away from him in another town. She lived there with her parents. He would go to see his son Youssef, travelling in a bus for miles and miles. They were long journeys and on the way the bus would stop on the wayside. The passengers would alight, fires would be lit and a whole sheep roasted on the spit. Everybody sat and ate as if they were in no haste to resume the journey. They sat around and waited patiently till the food was ready, ate and then proceeded on the journey.

Mohand had been brought up against a background of French colonialism. Yet, at home every evening the brothers would stand, ranged up against the wall reciting from the Quran, in loud voices which reverberated so that the neighbours could hear the fervour of their utterance. As a child he had wept because his mother had told him he was too young to begin fasting at Ramadan. Yet as he grew older he began to question his own beliefs. He liked to drink wine but it was forbidden in his culture. 'They would kill me' he said, 'if they knew I drank beer and wine.' He would describe the foetuses in the dust bins when spring came. He moved between two cultures, the Arabic and the French.

There was a Frenchman who had a house close to that of his family, with a magnificent library of French classical literature. One day he left hurriedly; this was the period when the French Colonials were beginning to leave North Africa. The period of colonial rule was coming to an end. Mohand and his brothers and friends went to the Frenchman's house and took volume after volume of French literature. But after some time the news came that the Frenchman was returning to his home. The police were coming to search for the books. Mohand's father told them, 'Bury the books, bury them'. They dug up holes and buried the books.

As a university student he had been involved in politics, deeply so. He too joined in the protest marches against the Establishment and was arrested and put into prison.

'Did you suffer?' I asked him.

'I did not stay as long as the others' he said.

'The prison was like a big dormitory in which we were housed. The warders were kind to us. But there are many students who are still in prison. As a teacher I would visit them and discuss their studies with them.'

Sometimes Mohand would sing Arabic songs. He would close his eyes to the Berber music on his cassette, his body swaying in trance-like movements, lost, his eyes half closed. He would talk of the Berber dancers, how they danced in a circle, moving the neck, the shoulders, the hips. Clapping their hands to the rhythm. 'They dance on and on,' he said.

'What does it mean?' I ask, 'all those dances.'

'Life' he replied, 'the cycle of life.'

We stand watching the snowflakes fall. Winter makes us vulnerable. We remain at the window and watch the landscape with its swirling snow feathers. The whole world begins to grow white, to lighten. The patterned icicles of my thoughts grow on the glass pane. We look out upon a hundred windows which turn blank faces towards us. Lives of strangers lie hidden behind the shuttered glass panes. Perhaps there are people watching our windows too, from behind the black faces of closed windows. Beyond us lies the City of the Dead with the elaborate towers and monuments which house dust and memory.

'I talk to myself,' he says, 'I look into the mirror and talk. You are *fou*, you are mad, I tell myself.' Angst. Despair. 'But what can I do? I am but myself, I cannot change.'

We are in another country. Each one of us brings our own landscapes into this winter-bound room in which we have our conversations. He brings the desert with the fortress of the Ksar and I bring my tropical garden which whirrs with cicada sounds, birds and insects. He leads me into the Ksar which rises out of the sands. Its towers grow tall and upwards, it does not extend into the oasis although there is plenty of fertile land outside. The fortress was made of mud bricks baked and baking in the sun. The river ran through the oasis. There were date palms, fruit trees, fields. The tallest house was the Caide's. During the day the peole leave the maze of rooms and passages in the Ksar and go out into the oasis to gather fuel, pluck fruit and gather grain. The Ksar that Mohand describes is in his father's village, the village of Little Horns, Tachioine. The tower in the desert is called Al-Nif. You have memories, so many of them, you lie on a carpet asleep beside your two aunts. Your uncle comes in and the two women push you aside to make

135

room for him. You feel cold, lonely. The loneliness always remains with you.

You tell me the story of Aicha Kandisha. She is a spirit which appears out of the darkness and lures you as you walk on a lonely road at night. As you tell me the story, a poem forms in my mind and I sit down at my writing desk one night and write it. I read it aloud to you one evening in this ice-bound city with the disembodied sounds of heels clicking sharply on pavements. My voice bore us into that country where you had once walked in fear and trembling, imagining that Aicha Kandisha would suddenly appear before you. I shared your fear as if we both had a kinship with those supernatural spirits that inhabited the darker worlds we moved within. Here too, there were ghosts walking these streets, but they were the disembodied spirits of ourselves, come back to haunt us. This then was the poem:

Walking through the void and the wilderness
Hood down, eyes filled with darkness
The monstrous trees in the sharp winds
Hurtle like stones about the silence
And the desert is wide, growing,
Growing like spectres of palms
Extending their flatness
She drifts out of the dark; Aicha Kandisha
Is fantastic in the amorousness of love
Drinks through the heart
The cup at her breast
And walks through your eyes,
Her heartbeat is thunder
In your veins
Walking through
The monstrous bat-dark into
Void where clinging hands
Give way.

How then were we to become friends among all these

strangers we lived among? We sat at those long polished tables, each with a tray of food before us. Tentatively we begin talking, looking at faces, searching for that first glimmer of kinship. Our hands reach out, grasp handles of cups, break bread, slice into food and eat, drink as if at a private mass, a consummation of our own sacrifice of flesh and blood. We complete our meal, leave scraps of broken meat and bread and a sup of milk, we rise from our seats and go in different directions, up stairways, lifts, along corridors, back to our rooms which we either share or occupy singly and open books, take up pens or peer through windows. A street full of shops lie on either side of the street. I know every one of them, especially the Bridal shop, the shop of dreams and illusions. People walk on the pavements briskly and purposefully as if they all have a destination they must quickly reach. From my window I see the Health shop with figures exercising, lifting weights, riding on bicycles, shaping their bodies. It is a ballet I see before me, the figures moving lithely in their black leotards. The smell of fish and chips creeps up from the shop where the oil sizzles and smokes in pans as the haggis, sausage, fish fry in their batter.

We leave the seclusion of our thoughts and our secret lives when we go down for breakfast and high tea. Sometimes we isolate a face among others and think 'Who is this man?' or 'Who is this woman?' Can we get close to any of them? Is there even time in this brief space that we share together. I notice a face. A man who sits at a faraway table. It is my first consciousness of Mohand. His face is a mask. Could he be from the Yemen? One of those Middle East countries? The skin is a dark olive, the forehead wide, the hair fits closely over the skull like a thick packed swarm of bees. His thoughts seem honeycomb pressed into his mind; eyes embedded in the skull, the jewelled light waiting to be released from the rough uncut stone that has just been mined and brought up from the gem pits, hard diamonds hewn out of seams of rock, or topazes with their fluid gold scintillate glitter or the wild yellow eyes of some wild cat or

137

panther? A look of abstraction makes his expression absent although he must be aware of everything and everyone around him, for we are all aware, alert, observing each other closely because the time must come when we have to make our choices of friends, whom we will spend our time talking to or walking with or sharing our thoughts and feelings with. Getting up and leaving the table, he gives me a slight bow with the merest inclination of his head. It was the wordless acceptance of another stranger who was still holding on to silence. We could not hold onto ourselves much longer. We were changing subtly in these new climes, the colour of our skins grew lighter, the texture of the hair, softer. Even the quality of language, so that our own voices became softer, more muted amidst the Babel of voices, the strange tongues and dialects that swirl about our ears.

He comes in from the cold street where music blares forth frenetically from the discos and the bars. The fish and chip shops are hazed over with blue clouds of smoke. In the bars, figures move with their reflections in the silvery mirrors which line the walls, a shimmering purgatory or paradise of bodies, which flow as if caught up in a world of blazing, exploding light. His breath has the faint aftermath of the drinking in lonely bars. He sits with his glass of beer which he loves, foaming over, savouring his solitary pleasure. Watching people. They watch him too. The Indian in one of the bars gets hot and angry with him because he thinks that his girl friend becomes too familiar with this stranger. He goes to the disco with Ahamed the Egyptian. His senses reel with the loud music and the flashing coloured lights, the air thick with smoke that suffocates you, jammed against the madly swirling bodies that are caught up in the loud thumping sounds of drums and the metallic steel strings of electric guitars. He is transfixed, transfigured, falling dizzy onto the floor which whirls round and round him, like pinwheels of light, that grow into large moving circles that widen and then contract. He walks to the bars alone and drinks. Then he returns to his room, opens a book, reads, locked in his consciousness. He tells me later, 'I am a man who is a lost soul.' He tells me that he tosses in his sleep and is wakeful. He tastes blood on his tongue. He thinks 'I am going to die. I have a cancer.'

We stand and talk, momentarily facing each other, suspended in this brief waiting before we went back to our private lives. He begins to tell me about his dream in the orchard.

'I was a soldier fighting in the walled orchard that lies below those windswept mountains in Midelt. My enemies were faceless. I heard the fury of battle in my ears yet I felt that even in the midst of all this fighting I must not die. I am surrounded on all sides, my enemies have an armoury of weapons, but I must fight on. I cannot understand why I am being fought against and in this strange conflict no one will ever emerge the final victor. I cannot say who wants to destroy me. Why do they look upon me as their enemy? Who will be the first among us to lay down arms and surrender? If I step outside the walled orchard I know that I can escape, but I am unable to move out of the battle fray, to step outside this fortress.'

The Atlas Mountains are always in his mind. It is here that the women too go to pick up their firewood. He tells me the story of one of these women. He admired her courage. She had gone to the mountains that morning and there she had given birth. That evening she had walked back to her home which lay several miles away carrying her child with her.

One evening I met him outside in the foyer of the hall. He was all wrapped up in his warm fur lined coat.

'You were not at High Tea this evening?' he smiled at my question.

'Perhaps there are other hungers that must be appeased' I said.

He passed off the disembodied teasing of my words without comment. Hungers. We were starving for warmth, for friendship, for affection. We were famished for a look, a gesture that would take us out of our frozen loneliness, the light whose faintest glimmer we tried to catch within the shuttered window of a lonely soul. Yet we were warm here, warm and fed and comfortable but we felt the chill that wrapped itself round the frozen heart. He searched for this warmth in those lighted bars that filled every street and then came back to watch endless programmes in the TV lounge, or to play pool or read for hours, working on his papers till the early hours of the morning and sleeping late.

One evening I see the little Syrian woman with the bright red lipstick daubed all over her lips standing by him near the Hall Porter's niche. He takes his card out of the slot and puts it back in its rightful place among the photographs of the other students. The visit is over. She used to come to his room where they read through their books, he on his seat at the writing desk and she at the other end. But she disturbs him, he tells me later. She wants to sing to him. She feels she has a beautiful voice, like a songbird. She writes poems, romantic verses about love which she wants to read to him. She has large white teeth that glisten when she opens her mouth. He admires their regularity but he cannot endure her insistent need for attention. He is not an unselfish man and one who will give attention only when he 'feels like to it', as he says. He admits that he is selfish, but he also comes from a very patriarchal society where women are not given too much freedom or attention, although he says that he is an exception and treats his wife differently. When he enter-tains his friends she does not have to spend time preparing the food, although he says that the women who come from her region are very good cooks. Yet it is obvious that he does what he wants with his life. He takes his tent and pitches it so that they have a vacation. Everybody comes, all his in-laws. Halfway through he says, 'I must be going soon. If you want you can continue your holiday.' His wife and he grow estranged. They separate. She lives with her family.

'If you are going away, you must give me two thousand pounds,' she says. She weeps and tells him that that is what her family want her to ask of him. Yet, now that he is here, in this country so far from his home, they write to each other, she in Arabic, he in French and she sends him a rich oily sweetmeat made of peanuts. He will go back to her because of Youssef and because of his baby daughter whom at first he had not wanted. The child he felt had been forced on him so that he would not leave his wife.

No, he could not get away, he could never escape or sever completely the very bonds that he sought every moment of his life to free himself from.

He shows me the picture of Youssef which he carries in his wallet. He loves his son deeply. 'He is of my blood, he is only six years, but he dances Flamenco when he hears Spanish music.' He takes him to watch bullfights in Spain; he can imitate the matadors. His wife spoils him but he loves his father more although he is more strict with him. We both talk compulsively of our children as if we want to feel their presence beside us in this lonely world. Yet I had been reluctant to make friends with anyone too closely. There were often discos in the hall and my friends would want me to come and join in the dancing. I had refused, preferring to stay in my room with the door shut, poring over my books or looking out on the world of Sauchiehall Street which lay below me. I once borrowed a book from Mohand, 'The Comfort of Strangers', when we had discovered that we belonged to the same department at the university. I had only stood at the door of his room with the door slightly ajar, unwilling to obtrude on his privacy. Privacy was something sacred here because you were surrounded by hundreds of other lives pursuing their different pastimes of pleasure or pain. You could hear them as they moved about, the clicking of heels, the opening and shutting of doors, the notes of a cello, the sound of a persistent cough, music on the cassettes, but your voice had to be low so as not to disturb your neighbour. Yet there was always loneliness which could drive some of the young ones even to thoughts of suicide. Others formed relationships which they were aware would never be permanent. But they were necessary, love or friendship, or you would be like the old, sad, lonely souls sitting in the warmth of the Savoy Centre staring silently into space, or sleeping in a cinema or sitting on a park bench for hours.

Yet we all knew that we were transients in this life, in this city, in this world. It was late spring when we met, the leaves were changing colour on the trees, soon the branches would be bare. White snow would cover the streets, the buildings and parks. But winter too would be over, spring and summer would follow and then it would be time for all of us to leave these landscapes which had grown to be so much a part of our lives, so familiar that we had ceased to even long for the sights and sounds and smells of our own countries. You carried my bags down and we said goodbye at the entrance of the hall. I remembered another line in your diary: 'Sometimes there's God suddenly.'

Death is not a decoration
Swords slash walls not flesh
Polished blood burns metal
The blade blunts not on
Bone but brick
Time has no hands
To hold these weapons
So they are put away   are soon forgotten
But death will stay
And we surmise that ghosts do battle

Other Titles from
the Indian subcontinent
Published by Forest Books

THE TWELFTH MAN

Poems by Iftikhar Arif

Translated from the Urdu by Brenda Walker

'Not enough attention has been paid to the poets of
the Indian subcontinent, among whom Iftikhar Arif is
a distinctive and memorable voice. Arif writes in Urdu.
Interestingly, though, his poems work extremely well
in English too. These poems belong to the modern
world and are acquainted with irony as much as
myth.' (Derek Mahon)

ISBN 0 948259 49 3   paper £6.95   96 pages
(dual text: Urdu/English)

THE TALISMAN

Stories & Poems by Ganga P. Vimal

Edited by Wendy Wright

Rich or poor, powerful or powerless, Ganga P. Vimal
asks questions about Indian society in lively stories
full of humour though always haunted by the presence
of death. His poems, inspired by the Himalayas,
tremble on a knife edge of reality and unreality.

ISBN 0 948259 57 4   paper £8.95   314 pages
(dual text: Hindi/English)

POETRY FROM BENGAL

Translated by Ron D.K. Banerjee

Unesco Library of World Poetry

In Bengal, where the poet is never far from the life of
the people, the mind searches for truth, as this selec-
tion shows, with all the agility of the ascetic and all the
brilliance of the fierce Indian sun.

ISBN 0 948259 79 5   paper £8.95   208 pages